HOMESPUN

HANDKNIT

CAPS SOCKS MITTENS & GLOVES

EDITED BY

LINDA LIGON

Library of Congress #87-80522
ISBN #0-934026-26-2
First printing: 15M:1187:AG/BB
Second printing: 8M:289:AG
Third printing: 18M:590:AG
Fourth printing: 5M:391:AG

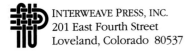 INTERWEAVE PRESS, INC.
201 East Fourth Street
Loveland, Colorado 80537

COVER: SIGNORELLA GRAPHIC ARTS

For mothers and grandmothers
who pass on their skills,
and especially for
Elizabeth Zimmermann,
the ''Mother of all''.

Acknowledgements

In addition to the *Spin·Off* contest winners whose designs appear here, I'd like to thank a very special group of knitters whose work I've long admired for responding to an invitation to contribute to this volume. They include Betty Amos, Janetta Dexter, Jackie Fee, Theresa Gaffey, Priscilla Gibson-Roberts, Robin Hansen, Beverly Royce, Jean Scorgie, Meg Swansen, Carol Thilenius, and last only by virtue of the alphabet, Elizabeth Zimmermann.

I'd also like to thank Mary Lamb Becker, for meticulously editing the project instructions; Ann Sabin, for styling many of the photos, drawing illustrations, and laying out pages; Joe Coca, for his fine photography; Marc Owens, for setting type (all those K 1's!), Michael Signorella, for a charming cover design; Deb Robson, for searching out endless little errors; and Karen Evanson, for keeping it all organized.

L.L.

Preface

This book was born amidst some good fun—a contest sponsored by *Spin·Off* Magazine in 1985. Spinners and knitters were invited to submit their favorite patterns for small projects; using handspun yarn wasn't a criterion, though many entrants did. The mail yielded a roomful of yummy, fuzzy, bright, wooly caps, scarves, mittens, gloves and socks for us to choose from. There were dear old favorites and funky experiments, sturdy everyday standbys and heirloom treasures.

What made all the pieces outstanding is that almost every one was thoughtfully designed and knitted with love for some particular person—a child, grandchild, spouse, friend, special customer. They were made to snug right down into someone's life. That's what makes knitting so wonderful. Commercially produced caps, socks, and mittens abound in the marketplace; but where can you find a cap that just matches your daughter's eyes, or gloves with cuffs that come up just so on your resident woodchopper's wrists? Or socks that make room for a funny second toe, or mittens so special that they will never languish in the lost-and-found?

The charm of knitting small projects like these is that they're portable, they *can* fit into your busy schedule, and they bring an indefinable pleasure every time they're worn. I hope you find patterns and ideas here that are just right for you, or the inspiration to make your own special changes. If you're a new knitter, I hope that seeing the endless variety in other knitters' work will give you the courage to experiment and personalize your own work, as knitters have been doing for centuries. Most of all, I hope you find hours of serenity and creative fun with your able hands, a continuous thread, and the ideas you find here.

Table of Contents

Needle Conversion Guidelines

Knitting needle size designations vary from one country to another, from one type to another, even from one brand to another. Variations might be a half-size or more. The following chart shows some equivalents, but the only way to be sure you have the right needle size is to make a gauge swatch.

American	Metric (mm)	British
00	2	14
0	2.25	13
1	2.5	12
2	2.75–3	11
3	3.25	10
4	3.5	9
5	3.75–4	8
6	4–4.5	7
7	4.5–5	6
8	5–5.5	5
9	5.5–6	4
10	6–6.5	3
10½	6.5–7	2
11	7–7.5	1
	8	0
13	8–8.5	00
15	8.5–9	000

Index to Special Techniques and Information

Some Approximations for Plain Yarns

These numbers are compiled from a variety of sources, from experience, and from the patterns in this book, none of which precisely agree! Use them as rough estimates only.

Yarn Style	Yds/lb	Approximate wraps/inch	Typical gauge	Approx. American needle size
lace	2600 +	18 +	8 +	00–2
fingering	1900–2400	16	6–8	2–4
sport	1200–1800	14	5–6½	4–6
worsted	900–1200	12	4–5	7–9
bulky	600–800	10	3–4	10–11
very bulky	400–500	8 or fewer	2–3	13–15

Introduction

IF YOUR KNITTING experience is mostly with commercial pattern booklets, this book will take some getting used to. First of all, it's a *kaffeeklatsch* of ideas—over three dozen knitters have contributed their favorite recipes. Some knitters think in charts, some think in lines—we've tried to retain each knitter's voice in translating her instructions to the printed page. So you can expect to find a technique—say a crown decrease—done one way one time, expressed a little differently another, and given a whole new approach on yet another design. Enjoy this diversity, and learn from it what you can. The chief message, I think, is that there's more than one way to skin a cat.

Choosing a Project

I assume you know the rudiments of knitting—knit, purl, yarn over, and so forth. This book will not teach you these things. But if *all* you know is, say, how to cast on and do a knit stitch, you'll find projects here that are not beyond you. Take note of the "beginner, intermediate, expert" notations at the beginning of each set of instructions, but don't let them keep you from trying. We just made those labels up based on our own ideas of what's hard. Look at the picture, read through the pattern and "knit it in your mind." You're the best judge of what you're ready to tackle. And given the modest size of most of these projects, you won't be risking a great deal if you get stuck.

Here are some fundamental techniques that have been used throughout the book, and a list of abbreviations. You'll find other tricks and techniques in the marginal notes as you read along.

Casting on

Choosing a cast-on technique is largely a matter of personal preference (or how your mother taught you), but some methods do tend to result in different degrees of stretch in the knitted edge. It's handy to know several cast-ons; here are three common ones, and you'll find other variations scattered throughout the book.

Simple one-needle cast-on (or long-tail cast-on): Measure off a length of yarn three or four times as long as your cast-on edge is to be, make a slip knot and place it on your needle. Hold the needle in your right hand, and the two yarn ends in the left as shown. Insert the point of the needle in the thumb loop, pick up the thread on your index finger, and draw it through the thumb loop. Drop the thumb loop and tighten the cast-on stitch on the needle. Repeat.

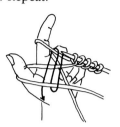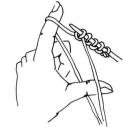

Twisted loop cast-on: This variation of the simple one-needle cast-on has a little more stretch—nice for the cuff of a cap, for instance. Measure off a length of yarn three to four times as long as your cast-on edge is to be. Hold the yarn tail in the left hand, and a needle and the strand coming off the ball in the right. Following the diagrams, pick up a loop off your thumb with your index finger, then knit that loop off your finger onto the needle. Repeat.

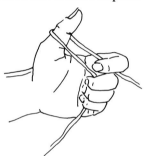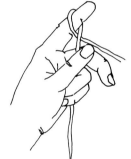

Two-needle cast-on, or cable cast-on: Make a slip knot near the end of your yarn, and place it on your left needle. Insert the right needle into the loop, and knit a stitch. Slip this knit stitch from the right needle onto the left needle. For the next stitch, insert the right needle *between* the two stitches that are now on the left needle, knit a stitch, and slip onto the left needle. Repeat.

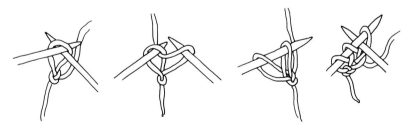

If your cast-on edges tend to be too tight, use a needle three or four sizes larger for casting on. If durability is a concern, as in a pair of mittens that's likely to wear out before it's outgrown, cast on with a double strand of yarn.

Increases

Simple increase: The most common increase, at least among American knitters, is worked by knitting a stitch, retaining that stitch on the left needle, and then knitting into the back of the same stitch before slipping them both to the right needle. This results in a little horizontal bar on the face of the fabric.

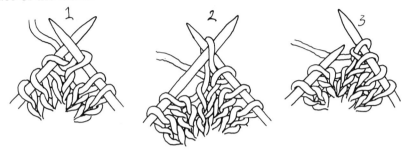

Make one: Several patterns in this book use the instruction "make 1" (M 1). In this context, it can mean one of two different techniques. The simplest is to make a backward loop on the right needle with your working yarn. This is especially useful if you need to make multiple increases all at once.

Raised increase: Some designers designate this type of increase as 'M 1', also. Using the left-hand needle, lift the horizontal thread between the two stitches that are on the two needles, and knit into it.

Invisible increase: An easy, unobtrusive increase that is similar to the raised increase. Knit one stitch into the stitch of the last row, then knit the next stitch on the left needle.

Decreases

The simplest decrease is **K 2 tog**, or knit two stitches together. This creates a decrease which slants to the right. To match it with a left-slanting decrease, slip one knitwise, knit one, and pass the slipped stitch over the knit stitch (**psso**). Another way to make a left-leaning decrease is to slip-slip-knit (**ssk**), for which you slip a stitch knitwise, slip a second stitch knitwise, and then insert the left needle into those two stitches and knit them off as one. This is a perfect mirror image of K 2 tog.

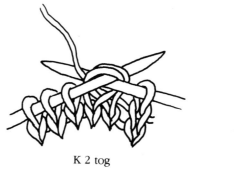

K 2 tog

ssk

Sl 1, k 1, psso

Yarn

Perhaps the greatest difference you'll find between this book and most knitting booklets and magazines is in the yarn specifications. Many of the patterns were created with handspun yarn, which has its own individual character that you're not likely to duplicate at your local yarn store, or even with your own yarn if you're a handspinner, too. That's okay. You'll find these guidelines given with each pattern to help you make substitutions:

• Yards per pound (and meters per kilogram). If you're a handspinner, you can use a McMorran Yarn Balance (see Resource Guide) to check your yardage. If you're buying commercial yarn, you can usually figure out the yardage from the specifications given on the label, with a little arithmetic or the help of your friendly shop owner. Yards per pound is not an infallible guide for yarn substitutions, though. Some yarns are more dense and tightly spun than others, and will therefore give different stitch gauges and different fabric quality.

• Wraps per inch (and wraps per 4 centimeters). This number indicates how many times you can wrap your yarn around a ruler (or other measure) in a given distance. It's a somewhat arbitrary measure, because some people wrap tighter than other people do.

• Yarn description. This includes whether it's a single, two, four or more ply; fiber content, and if it's handspun, what kind of wool or other fiber it includes; brand name and style if it's a commercial yarn other than a standard type.

• Suggested substitutes. In the case of handspuns, I've tried to indicate which standard knitting yarn they resemble—lace or fingering, sport, knitting worsted, bulky. This doesn't absolve you from making a gauge swatch, though!

The main thing to remember in choosing or spinning yarns for these projects is that you have some latitude. Put two fine yarns together to make a fatter one, change needle size, fudge the number of stitches a little —your nice stretchy knit fabric will forgive small adjustments. Do, however, make a gauge swatch, and make it every time you use a new yarn, or a new stitch. Not only will it save you from major misfits, it will give you the opportunity to create just exactly the fabric that you want, with whatever yarn you've chosen.

McMorran Yarn Balance

This is a simple but accurate device for figuring how many yards per pound in a given yarn. You simply drape a piece of yarn over the balance arm, and snip it shorter until the arm balances. Then measure the piece and multiply times 100—voila! Yards per pound! See Resource Guide for source.

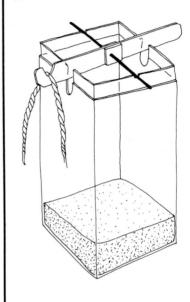

A Classic Mohair Tam, *Joy Hagler*

T HREE YEARS AGO, Joy Hagler and her friend Linda, both weavers, opened a shop called Loose Ends in Carbondale, Illinois. It soon became apparent that knitting was what their customers were most interested in, so they set about stocking the appropriate yarns and supplies—although neither of them knew how to knit. They soon learned.

The primary motive for designing a mohair beret, Joy says, was economics. "I insist on trying to run a high quality knitting and weaving shop in a financially depressed area. Finding myself with a great deal of mohair on hand and a clientele which dearly covets what it can rarely afford, this reinvention of the classic beret was the perfect choice for a low-budget indulgence.

"Although tams were very much in fashion, I couldn't find a suitable pattern. Undaunted, I finally succeeded after three most intense attempts, the first of which resembled a small, fuzzy laundry bag rather than a fashionable head cover.

"The final outcome was a huge success. Not only did I sell all but two of the many I produced, and many do-it-yourself kits for my customers, I also proved that with a little persistence, even an amateur knitter like myself can produce beautiful, original wearables."

Joy's tam requires only one 50-gram skein of mohair blend yarn, and knits up quickly at 4 stitches per inch.

For the beginning knitter.

Size: Adult average. Changes for a wider tam (not bigger in cuff diameter) follow in parentheses.

Yarn: 960 yd/lb (2016 m/kg). Joy used 1 50 g (1¾ oz) skein of brushed mohair from Ironstone Warehouse.

Gauge: With larger needles over stockinette st 4 sts = 1 in (16 sts = 10 cm).

Needles: Circular needles, 16 in (40 cm) length, sizes 7 (4.5-5 mm, 6) and 9 (5.5-6 mm, 4) or size to reach gauge given above; one set dpn in larger size.

Instructions: With smaller needles cast on 78 sts. Work in k 1, p 1 rib for 1¼ in (3.2 cm). Change to larger needles and st st.

Rnd 1: (K 12, inc in next st) 6 times—84 sts.

Rnd 2: Work even.

Rnd 3: (K 13, inc in next st) 6 times—90 sts.

Rnd 4: Work even.

Continue to inc 6 sts every other rnd as above 3 (4) times more, working 1 more st bet incs on each inc rnd—108 (114) sts. Work even until total length measures 4 in (10 cm).

Top shaping: Rnd 1: [K 16 (17), k 2 tog] 6 times—102 (108) sts.

Rnd 2: Work even.

Rnd 3: [K 15 (16), k 2 tog] 6 times—96 (102) sts.

Rnd 4: Work even. Continue to dec 6 sts every other rnd as above 5 (6) times more, having 1 fewer st bet decs on each dec rnd and working even on rnds following dec rnd. Change to dpn when number of sts requires it. When 66 sts remain and last work even rnd is completed, dec 6 sts *every* rnd until 6 sts rem. Run tail through and fasten securely on underside.

Handwritten marginal notes:

÷ circum. by π (3.14) = Diam.

Jane's mohair tam: worked to 144 sts. (24 sts/section) — nice shape! Make again! (used 2 - 50g. / 1¾ oz. hanks of mohair - 98 yds ea.) Use balance of yarn to make sm. neck scarf. size 13 needles - cast on 16 sts. Worked K2 P2 til near end. Work 6 sts., cast off 4, loop 4, cont. work. 6 sts. Work next row. Then K 2 tog. both ends every row for sev. rows. Run end of yarn thru remain. sts. sev. time & knot.

Jorn /blue, wool/silk tam: worked to 24 sts/section (144 sts)

CLASSIC MOHAIR TAM

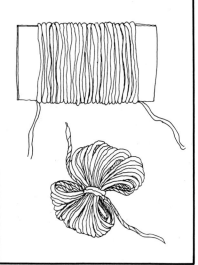
A Basic Hemmed Hat, *Sidna Farley*

SIDNA FARLEY OF Denver, Colorado, has been knitting for twenty-five years, and teaching for twelve. She's been designing her own sweaters for over a decade, and her original designs have appeared in *Knitters* magazine. Sidna is especially fond of projects that can be knitted in the round because "I like to knit, not sew things up."

"My hemmed hat is not unusual or fancy," Sidna says, "but it's a good basic hat. It's the type I make most often for my family and is especially good for teenagers, as they like hats that look similar to everyone else's. For a while, I made a new hat for each new jacket."

The crown of Sidna's hat can be shaped with a circular decrease, like the striped one shown here, or with a triangular crown like the "Woven Stitch" version on page 23. Using an invisible cast-on eliminates hemming, so the cap is ready to wear right off the needles.

For the intermediate knitter.

Size: Adult medium.

Yarn: 1000 yd/lb (2100 m/kg), 12 wraps/in (19/4 cm). Sidna used 4-ply knitting worsted, about 3 oz (85 gm) each of white and navy blue, and a small amount of green for the stripe and pompon.

Gauge: Over stockinette st 18 or 19 sts = 4 in (10 cm). Either works well; the hat will be slightly larger at 18 sts.

Needles: Circular needle, 16 in (40 cm) length, and one set of dpn, both size 7 (4.5-5 mm, 6) or size needed to knit to required gauge.

Instructions: With circular needle cast on 90 sts using invisible cast-on (page 21). Turn and knit back one row. Join and continue knitting around until 5½ or 6 in (14 cm) are completed.

Hem rnd: Sl sts from cast-on string to a second circular needle (size or length not important, but a smaller needle will slip in more easily); remove the string. Alternate stitches will be twisted on needle; either reposition them before beginning hem or knit into back lp as they are worked. Fold work with wrong sides together (second needle will be on inside). Knit first st of outside needle and first st of inside needle together. Continue around, knitting one st from outside needle tog with one st from inside needle until all sts are joined and hem is completed. Don't be concerned if you have an extra st. If it's on the inside needle, drop it. If it's on the outside needle, knit it.

For stripe, knit 2 rnds green. Change to navy blue and work until length from fold line of hem is 7 in (18 cm).

Decrease for top: Rnd 1: (K 13, k 2 tog, place marker) 6 times.

Rnd 2 and all following rnds: * K to 2 sts before marker, k 2 tog; rep from * until 6 sts rem, changing to dpn when sts no longer slide comfortably around circular needle.

Break yarn and run through sts. Finish, adding white and green pompon if you wish.

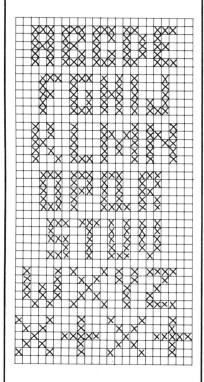

Three Flower Hat, *Sidna Farley*

THE SHAPE of this basic cap lends itself to almost any kind of patterning you can dream up, from simple stripes to expert stitches like this "Three Flower" one. In this version, Sidna has worked her daughter's initials along with other geometric motifs, and topped it off with an unusual and challenging pattern stitch from Barbara Walker's *A Second Treasury of Knitting Patterns.* You'll find a very different version of the same basic shape on page 26, Northern Lights Bohus Hat.

For the expert knitter.

Size: Adult medium.

Yarn: 1000 yd/lb (2100 m/kg), 12 wraps/in (19/4 cm). Sidna used 4-ply knitting worsted, about 2 oz (57 g) each of white and green, and a small amount of red knitting worsted weight yarn.

Gauge: Over stockinette st 19 sts = 4 in (10 cm).

Needles: Circular needle, 16 in (40 cm) length, and one set of dpn, both size 7 (4.5-5 mm, 6) or size to reach gauge given above.

Instructions: With green and circular needle cast on 80 sts. Working back and forth, knit 10 rows (5 ridges) garter st. (Editor's note: If you prefer, you can work 10 *rnds* of garter st: K 1 rnd, p 1 rnd. This will eliminate the need for seaming these first 10 rows later.)

Next row: Knit, increasing 10 sts evenly spaced—90 sts. Join work and change to st st. Work even 3 rnds.

Make chart for initials: Allowing 90 squares of graph paper to represent 90 sts, plan pattern using 5 lines (rows). Fill in rem spaces with "X"s or "+"s or your own design. Work next 5 rnds from chart using white for contrast color. (Editor's note: If yarn must be carried more than 3 or 4 sts, twist yarn being carried around yarn being worked to prevent long floats on wrong side.) When chart is completed, work 3 rnds with green. Beg Three Flower pat (worked over a multiple of 10 sts):

Rnd 1: With green, * p 4, p 3, wrapping yarn 3 times for each st, p 3; rep from * around.

Rnd 2: With white * sl 1 with yarn in back (wyib), k 3, sl 3 wyib dropping extra wraps, k 3; rep from * around.

Rnd 3: With white, * sl 1 wyib, k 3, sl 3 wyib, k 3; rep from * around.

Rnds 4 and 5: With white, k 4, * sl 3 wyib, k 7; rep from * around to last 6 sts end sl 3 wyib, k 3.

Rnd 6: With white, k 2, * sl 2 wyib, drop next (first green) st off needle and put in front of work, sl same 2 sl sts back to left needle, pick up dropped st and knit it; k 3, drop next (3rd green) st off needle and put in front of work, k 2, pick up dropped st and knit it, ** k 3; rep from * around to last 8 sts, work from * to **, k 1.

Rnd 7: With red, sl 2 wyib, * [(k 1, p 1, k 1) in next st, sl 2 wyib] twice, (k 1, p 1, k 1) in next st, ** sl 3 wyib; rep from * around to last 8 sts, work from * to **, sl 1 wyib.

Rnd 8: With red sl 2 wyib, * make bobble (MB) in next 3 (increased) sts as follows: P 3, turn, k 3, turn, sl 1, k 2 tog, psso—bobble completed; (sl 2 wyib, MB) twice, ** sl 3 wyib; rep from * around to last 14 sts, work from * to **, sl 1 wyib.

Rnd 9: With white k, working into back of each bobble st. Continue with white until hat is 6 in (15 cm) from the beginning.

Top shaping: Rnd 1: (K 13, sl 1, k 1, psso, place marker) 6 times. **Rnd 2 and all following rnds:** * K to 2 sts before marker, sl 1, k 1, psso; rep from * until 6 sts remain, changing to dpn when sts no longer slide comfortably around circular needle. Break yarn and run through sts. Finish and sew seam in band (unless band was worked in rnds).

Invisible Cast-on

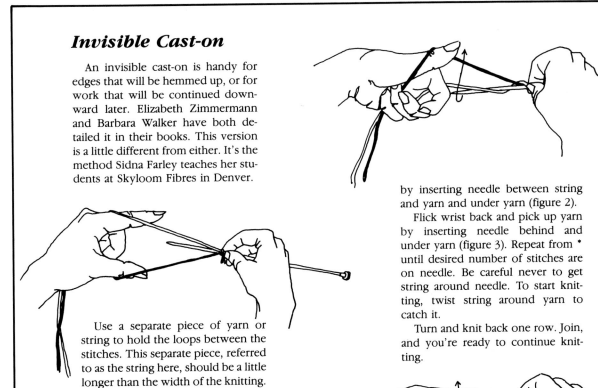

An invisible cast-on is handy for edges that will be hemmed up, or for work that will be continued downward later. Elizabeth Zimmermann and Barbara Walker have both detailed it in their books. This version is a little different from either. It's the method Sidna Farley teaches her students at Skyloom Fibres in Denver.

Use a separate piece of yarn or string to hold the loops between the stitches. This separate piece, referred to as the string here, should be a little longer than the width of the knitting. Tie the string to the yarn.

Hold needle in right hand with knot toward you and thumb over knot. Hold both yarn and string in left hand in same way as for long-tail casting on, with yarn over forefinger and string over thumb (figure 1).

*Turn wrist back and down so palm is facing you. Yarn is down behind and under string. Pick up yarn by inserting needle between string and yarn and under yarn (figure 2).

Flick wrist back and pick up yarn by inserting needle behind and under yarn (figure 3). Repeat from * until desired number of stitches are on needle. Be careful never to get string around needle. To start knitting, twist string around yarn to catch it.

Turn and knit back one row. Join, and you're ready to continue knitting.

Woven Stitch Hat, *Sidna Farley*

THIS VARIATION of Sidna's Basic Hemmed Hat, page 18, has a tricky and distinctive pattern stitch and a triangular decrease at the crown. The pattern stitch is collected in many knitting books, including Barbara Walker's *Treasury of Knitting Patterns*. Sidna has rewritten it for circular knitting.

For the intermediate knitter.

Size: Adult medium.

Yarn: 1000 yd/lb (2100 m/kg), 12 wraps/in (19/4 cm). Sidna used 4-ply knitting worsted, about 2 oz (170 g) of tan, and 1 oz (28 g) each of red and blue.

Gauge: Over stockinette st 18 or 19 sts = 4 in (10 cm).

Needles: Circular needle, 16 in (40 cm) length, and one set of dpn, both size 7 (4.5-5 mm, 6) or size to reach above gauge.

Instructions: With circular needle and tan cast on 90 sts using invisible cast-on (page 21). Turn and knit back one row. Join and continue knitting around until 5½ to 6 in (15 cm) are knit.

Hem rnd: Sl lps from cast-on string to a second circular needle (size or length not important, but a smaller needle will slip in more easily); remove the string. Alternate stitches will be twisted on needle. Either reposition them before beginning hem or knit into back lp of twisted sts as they are worked. Fold work with wrong sides together (second needle will be on inside). Knit first st of outside needle and first st of inside needle together. Continue around, knitting one st from outside needle tog with one st from inside needle until all sts are joined and hem is completed. Don't be concerned if you have an extra st. If it's on the inside needle, drop it. If it's on the outside needle, knit it.

Begin pat st as follows: Woven pat st (worked over even number of sts):

Rnd 1: With tan, knit.

Rnd 2: With red, * sl 1 with yarn in front (wyif), k 1; rep from * around.

Rnd 3: With red, knit.   **Rnd 4:** With blue, * k 1, sl 1 wyif; rep from * around.

Rnd 5: With blue, knit.   **Rnd 6:** With tan, * sl 1 wyif, k 1; rep from * around.

Rnd 7: With tan, knit.   **Rnd 8:** With red, * k 1, sl 1 wyif; rep from * around.

Rnd 9: With red, knit.

Rnd 10: With blue, * sl 1 wyif, k 1; rep from * around.

Rnd 11: With blue, knit.

Rnd 12: With tan, * k 1, sl 1 wyif; rep from * around.

Rnd 13: With tan, knit. Rep Rows 2-13 for pat.

Continue in pat stitch until length from fold of hem is 7 in (18 cm). End pat stitch.

Begin triangular dec: Mark first and 46th sts. * K to st before marked st, sl 2 tog as to knit, k 1, p2sso; rep from * until there are 4 sts left, changing to dpn when sts no longer slide comfortably around circular needle. Break yarn and run through sts.

Hooded Scarf, *Joan Steskal*

ABOUT TWENTY YEARS ago, Joan Steskal's husband gave her a hooded scarf that had been machine knitted in a Scandinavian country. She has recreated it for us because it's so very easy to knit, yet pretty and practical.

Joan, who lives in Rancho Palos Verdes, California, was taught to knit by her grandmother while in grammar school. But it's handspinning that has made her a constant knitter. "I love the feel of handspun," she says. "I always have a sweater in progress for one of my five children, and my knitting goes with me everywhere—to work, on short and long trips, to appointments, wherever I can sit and my hands will be free for five minutes or more."

The yarn in Joan's hood is an exceptionally soft, lightweight two-ply, spun from an Australian Border Leicester fleece blended with angora. It's dyed a soft, lovely blue with indigo. She scanned her pattern books for a pattern that looked equally attractive on both sides and had a multiple of less than ten (so she could have at least four repeats).

For the beginning knitter.

Size: Approximately 9 in x 55 in (23 cm x 140 cm).

Yarn: 900 yd/lb (1890 m/kg), 12 wraps/in (19/4 cm). Joan used 6 oz (170 g) of her own handspun yarn, a blend of 90% wool and 10% angora. A 4-ply knitting worsted type yarn could be substituted.

Gauge: Over pat st 23 sts = 4 in (10 cm).

Needles: Single-pointed needles, size 5 (3.75-4 mm, 8) or size to reach gauge given above; crochet hook size F or 5 (4 mm, 8).

Instructions: Cast on 43 sts and work in following pattern:

Pattern stitch: Seeded Rib Check (multiple of 4 sts plus 3)

    Row 1: K 3, * p 1, k 3; rep from * across.

    Row 2: K 1, * p 1, k 3; rep from * across to last 2 sts, end p 1, k 1.

    Rows 3 and 5: Rep Row 1.

    Rows 4 and 6: Rep Row 2.

    Rows 7, 9 and 11: Rep Row 2.

    Rows 8, 10 and 12: Rep Row 1. Rep Rows 1-12 for pat, working even until length measures approximately 54 in. or longer if desired. Bind off.

Finishing: Fold in half horizontally with wrong sides together. Sew edges together on one side from fold down for 9 in (23 cm).

To sew: With strand of scarf yarn go from bump to bump, and bar to bar. Go through the bumps and just under top strand of bar so as not to form ridge. Single crochet all around edges. At the corners of the scarf ends crochet 3 sts in same corner st to keep edging flat. On the cast-on and bind-off edges crochet in each st, but on the long sides crochet in every other row, in each bar, passing over the bumps.

Choosing an Appropriate Needle Size

Unless you always work with standard and consistent types of yarn like good old four-ply knitting worsted, you probably often face the quandary of deciding what size needle to choose. Here's Joan Steskal's rule of thumb:

Choose a needle size that is equal to two strands of yarn. Double the yarn and hold it up behind the holes of a needle gauge. The largest hole that's completely covered is the size to try first.

Of course, to be sure your fabric will have just exactly the density and hand you want, you must work gauge samples, preferably at least 4 inches (10 cm) square, and over the stitch that will make the main body of your piece. Even if you think your first gauge is just fine, it's wise (and educational) to knit samples using needles one or more sizes larger and smaller.

Some knitters find that their gauge for flat work is different than that for the same stitch worked in the round. So be sure to check your gauge carefully after you've worked a few inches on circular needles, and make sure it matches your gauge swatch.

Northern Lights Bohus Hat, *Sidna Farley*

THE BOHUS STYLE of pattern knitting, which uses purl and slip stitches along with color stranded patterns to give the effect of more than two colors in a row, was pioneered in Sweden in the 1940's by Emma Jacobsson and the Bohus Knitting Cooperative. Elizabeth Zimmermann and Meg Swansen have written about it in *Wool Gathering* (number 26), and the Swedish book *Bohus Stickning* provides inspiring designs in this method.

This is a pattern Sidna developed for her beginner classes, so though the hat looks wonderfully complex, it's a tried and true simple introduction to this fascinating technique.

For the intermediate knitter.

Size: Adult medium.

Yarn: 1200 yd/lb (2520 m/kg), 14 wraps/in. Sidna used a firmly twisted 2-ply sportweight yarn from Condon, 2 oz (57 g) black and small amounts of royal blue, purple, fuchsia, cardinal, rust, and orange.

Gauge: Over stockinette st 22 sts = 4 in (10 cm).

Needles: Circular needles 16 in (40 cm) length, and one set of dpn, both in size 3 (3.25 mm, 10) to 5 (3.75–4 mm, 8) or size to reach gauge above.

Instructions: With circular needle and black cast on 98 sts. Work back and forth in garter st for 12 rows (6 ridges). Join work. (Editor's note: If you prefer, you can join and work first 12 rnds in garter st, i.e., k 1 rnd, p 1 rnd, which will eliminate need to seam band later.) Inc 14 sts evenly spaced around as follows: (k 7, work backward lp on right needle) 14 times—112 sts. Work even 2 rnds.

Begin pattern stitch using following instructions, or reading from chart. Note that the pattern stitch is primarily st st with a few purled and slipped sts.

Rnds 1, 2 and 3: K 2 black, * k 1 blue, k 3 black; rep from * around to last 2 sts, end k 1 blue, k 1 black.

Rnd 4: K 1 black, * p 1 blue, k 1 blue, p 1 blue, k 1 black; rep from * around to last 3 sts, end p 1 blue, k 1 blue, p 1 blue.

Rnd 5: K 1 black, * k 3 blue, k 1 black; rep from * around to last 3 sts, end k 3 blue.

Rnd 6: * P 1 blue, k 3 blue; rep from * around.

Rnd 7: * K 1 purple, k 3 blue; rep from * around.

Rnd 8: * K 1 purple, p 1 purple, k 1 blue, p 1 purple, k 1 purple, k 3 blue; rep from * around.

Rnd 9: K 6 purple, * k 1 blue, k 7 purple; rep from * around to last 2 sts, end k 1 blue, k 1 purple.

Rnd 10: * P 1 black, k 3 purple, p 1 black, k 1 purple, sl 1, k 1 purple; rep from * around.

Rnd 11: * Sl 1, k 1 purple, k 1 blue, k 1 purple, sl 1, k 3 purple; rep from * around.

Rnd 12: K 2 purple, * p 1 fuchsia, k 3 purple, k 1 fuchsia, k 3 purple; rep from * around to last 6 sts, end p 1 fuchsia, k 3 purple, k 1 fuchsia, k 1 purple.

NORTHERN LIGHTS BOHUS HAT

Rnd 13: K 2 purple, * k 1 fuchsia, k 3 purple, ; rep from * around to last 2 sts, end k 1 fuchsia, k 1 purple.

Rnds 14 and 15: * K 1 purple, k 3 fuchsia; rep from * around.

Rnd 16: * Sl 1, k 1 fuchsia, k 1 cardinal, k 1 fuchsia; rep from * around.

Rnd 17: * K 1 purple, k 1 fuchsia, sl 1, k 1 fuchsia; rep from * around.

Rnd 18: K 2 fuchsia, * k 1 cardinal, k 3 fuchsia; rep from * around to last 2 sts, end k 1 cardinal, k 1 fuchsia.

Rnd 19: * K 1 fuchsia, k 3 cardinal; rep from * around.

Rnd 20: * Sl 1, k 1 cardinal, k 1 black, k 1 cardinal; rep from * around.

Rnd 21: K 2 cardinal, * p 1 rust, k 3 cardinal, k 1 rust, k 3 cardinal; rep from * around to last 6 sts, end p 1 rust, k 3 cardinal, k 1 rust, k 1 cardinal.

Rnd 22: K 2 cardinal, * k 1 rust, k 3 cardinal; rep from * around to last 2 sts, end k 1 rust, k 1 cardinal.

Rnds 23 and 24: * K 1 cardinal, k 3 rust; rep from * around.

Rnd 25: * Sl 1, k 1 rust, k 1 orange, k 1 rust; rep from * around.

Rnd 26: * K 1 cardinal, sl 1, k 1 orange, sl 1; rep from * around.

Rnds 27 and 28: * K 1 cardinal, k 3 rust; rep from * around.

Rnd 29: * L 1 orange, k 1 cardinal, sl 1, k 1 cardinal; rep from * around.

Rnd 30: K 1 orange, p 1 orange, * k 1 rust, p 1 orange, k 1 orange, p 1 orange; rep from * around to last 2 sts, end k 1 rust, p 1 orange.

Rnd 31: K 2 orange, * k 1 rust, k 3 orange; rep from * around to last 2 sts, end k 1 rust, k 1 orange.

Rnd 32: K 1 black, sl 1, * k 1 rust, sl 1, k 1 black, sl 1; rep from * around to last 2 sts, end k 1 rust, sl 1.

Rnds 33 and 34: K 2 orange, * k 1 rust, k 3 orange; rep from * around to last 2 sts, end k 1 rust, k 1 orange.

Rnd 35: K 2 orange, * p 1 black, k 3 orange; rep from * around to last 2 sts, end p 1 black, k 1 orange.

Rnd 36: * K 1 orange, p 1 black, k 1 black, p 1 black; rep from * around.

Rnd 37: * K 1 black, k 1 orange, k 5 black, k 1 orange; rep from * around.

Rnd 38: K 2 black, * k 1 orange, k 3 black; rep from * around to last 2 sts, end k 1 orange, k 1 black.

Rnd 39: K 3 black, * k 1 orange, k 1 black, k 1 orange, k 5 black; rep from * around to last 5 sts, end k 1 orange, k 1 black, k 1 orange, k 2 black.

Rnd 40: K 4 black, * k 1 orange, k 7 black; rep from * around to last 4 sts, end k 1 orange, k 3 black.

Work 2 rnds black.

Top shaping: Rnd 1: * (K 17, k 2 tog, place marker) twice, k 18, place marker; rep from *—108 sts.

Rnd 2 and following rnds: * (K to 2 sts before marker, k 2 tog; rep from * until 6 sts rem, changing to dpn when sts no longer slide comfortably around circular needle. Break yarn and run through sts. Finish and sew seam in border (unless garter st was worked in rnds).

Legend:

- slip
- purl (in color indicated)
- black
- blue
- purple
- fuchsia
- red (cardinal)
- orange (rust)
- yellow-orange (orange)

Easy Upside Down Hat, *Dorothy Petersen*

THIS HAT and the Simply Dressy Hat (page 32) are both knit as straight tubes from the top down. Dorothy Petersen of Brookside, New Jersey, has developed this quick and easy pattern for her daughter, "a graphic designer working in the steel canyons of New York City, who can never seem to find winter hats that fit properly or are warm enough."

Dorothy has been knitting since she was eight years old, when her mother taught her during a seige of mumps. "Now I am back to knitting up a storm again since I have been laid up for the last nine months with a badly broken ankle," she says. "Needless to say, everyone received sweaters for Christmas this year!"

For the beginning knitter.

Size: Adult medium.

Yarn: 2250 yd/lb (4522 m/kg), 18 wraps/in (28/4 cm). Dorothy used Daphne from Tahki Imports, a fingering-weight 3-ply blend of silk and wool. She used a double strand throughout. Her hat required 4 25-g balls.

Gauge: With double strand of yarn and larger needle over stockinette st 5 sts = 1 in (20 sts = 10 cm); 13 rows = 2 in (13 rows = 5 cm).

Needles: 1 set each Size 6 (4-4.5 mm, 7) and 8 (5-5.5 mm, 5) dpn, or size to reach gauge given above.

Instructions: Yarn is used double throughout. Beginning at the crown, cast on 114 sts with larger needle and join without twisting stitches. Work in st st until work measures 8 in (20 cm). Dec 12 sts evenly spaced on next row—102 sts. Change to smaller needles and work in k 1, p 1 rib for 3½ in (9 cm). Cast off in ribbing very loosely using the larger needle to keep the cast-off elastic.

Sew top edge closed. Flatten this seam, forming triangles at each end of seam. Bring points of triangles together, and fasten securely with a pompon. Turn up ribbing to form cuff.

EASY UPSIDE DOWN HAT AND REVERSIBLE HEADBAND

Double Reversible Headband,

Joan Kozak

JOAN KOZAK of Hayward, Wisconsin, has been spinning and dyeing with plants for a dozen years, but "with children, building a house, etc., there's never as much time as I'd like," she says. While waiting for a house big enough for her weaving loom, Joan satisfies her fiber urges by knitting hats. She raises Angora rabbits and has two large, furry dogs, all of whom contribute to her soft, fluffy handspun yarns.

Odd scraps of a variety of richly colored wools make the outer layer of this snug headband, and a soft, soft wool angora blend on the inside keep the ears warm.

For the beginning knitter.

Size: Adult medium.

Yarn: 450 yd/lb (900 m/kg), 6-8 wraps/in (9-12/4 cm). Joan used irregular handspun wool about the size of Reynolds Lopi. The outside layer is about an ounce of mixed yarns, and the inside an ounce of soft, angora-like handspun doghair.

Gauge: Over stockinette st, 7 sts = 2 in (14 sts = 10 cm).

Needles: Circular needle, 16 in (40 cm) length, size 10 (6-6.5 mm, 3) or size to reach gauge given above.

Instructions: With circular needle and softer yarn cast on 44 sts very loosely. Knit until 4 in (10 cm) wide. Purl 1 rnd. Change to wool yarn. Continue knitting changing colors at random until 1 row short of 4 in (10 cm) from the p rnd. Change back to soft yarn; k 1 rnd. Tuck in loose ends. Fold softer half up inside second half. Pick up first cast-on st and sl to left needle, k 2 tog. * Pick up next cast-on st and sl to left needle, k 2 tog; pass previous st over last st worked to bind off. Rep from * across until all sts are bound off, working at a very loose tension.

Simply Dressy Hat, *Dorothy Petersen*

CAN YOU BELIEVE that this is the same hat as the blue one on page 30? Dorothy Petersen has chosen a nubbly yarn, turned her tube inside out for a reverse stockinette surface, and done a clever fold with the crown points. It's that simple.

For the beginning knitter.

Size: Adult medium.

Yarn: 500 yd/lb (1005 m/kg), 6 wraps/in (9/4 cm). Dorothy used a nubby ratine-type yarn, Paton's Topaz wool-acrylic blend. She used 3 50-g balls.

Gauge: With larger needle over stockinette st 7 sts = 2 in (14 sts = 10 cm); 5 rows = 1 in (8 rows = 4 cm).

Needles: Circular needle, 16 in (40 cm) length, or dpn, size 9 (5.5–6 mm, 4) or size to reach gauge given above; circular needle, 16 in (40 cm) length, or dpn, size 7 (4.5–5 mm, 6).

Instructions: When you knit with nubby yarns, the nubs tend to stay on the purl side. To take advantage of this, Dorothy turned the finished hat inside out so that the purl (nubby) side is on the outside. Like her Easy Upside Down Hat (page 30), this hat is knitted from the crown down.

Cast on 80 sts with larger needle and join without twisting sts. Work in st st (all knit since you are working in the round), for 11 in (28 cm). On the next rnd dec 6 sts evenly spaced around—74 sts. Change to smaller needles and work k 1, p 1 rib for 3 in (8 cm). Bind off very loosely in ribbing using the larger needle to avoid having a restricting edge.

Sew top edge closed; turn hat inside out. Flatten top seam, forming triangles at each end of seam. Bring points of triangles together, then fold both triangles to one side of hat. Turn up ribbing to form cuff. Bring closer triangle down to just touch edge of the band. Tack in place using button, pompon or tassel if desired.

stitch

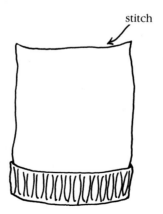

Birds and Bees Cap, *Nancy Spates Minton*

SEVERAL JOYFUL EVENTS led to this little cap," writes Nancy Minton of Lansing, Michigan. "Thinking about a friend expecting a springtime baby while laughing with my own toddler as hungry birds landed at our windowsill amidst the bleakness of a Michigan January. With drab skies and white surroundings, those haughty jays somehow lifted the 'blues'.

"One thing led to another and I realized a 'spring birds and bees' cap in handspun, natural colors was the gift I wanted to make for my friend. Perhaps at our best, motherhood gives us wings to fly, too, and I hope that for my friend. And I hope, a humorous gift from me, a pediatrician, to my friend, a child psychiatrist."

Nancy's cap is based on a traditional design that she found in *Kids' Knits* by Lesley Anne Price. She has visions of a future cap with robins, finches, cardinals, thrushes, chickadees if she can figure out how to do it with only two colors per row! And she's also done a "Hansel and Gretel" version for her own daughter. "This basic pattern lends itself easily to innovation and fun," she says.

Nancy's yarns were handspun and dyed with natural dyes by Jamie Harmon. "The handmade quality of the wool added tremendously to my pleasure in creating but I'll never find the time to spin, dye *and* knit in this lifetime."

For the intermediate knitter.

Size: 3- to 7-year-old child.

Yarn: 550 yd/lb (1005 m/kg), 13 wraps/in (20/4 cm). Nancy used an irregular handspun wool, similar in weight and texture to a Tahki Designer Tweed. Her hat uses 150 yd (180 m) or 2¾ oz (78 g) of natural white, and 7 20-yd (24 m) lengths of rainbow pastels.

Gauge: Over stockinette st 6 sts = 1 in (9 sts = 4 cm); 8 rnds = 1 in (12 rows = 4 cm).

Needles: One set of dpn, size 3 (3.25 mm, 10) or size to reach gauge given above. Optional, for cord ties and border: Circular needle, size 3 (3.25 mm, 10), and two dpn, size 2 (2.75-3 mm, 11). If crocheted ties and border are substituted: crochet hook, size F or 5 (4 mm, 8).

Instructions: With Size 3 dpn and white cast on 128 sts. Divide on 3 needles and join, being careful not to twist sts. Work in st st for 4 rnds. Follow graph A for Rnds 5-25.

Rnd 26: (K 1, k 2 tog) 3 times, (k 5, k 2 tog) 17 times—108 sts.

Rnds 27-33: Follow graph A for flying bird motif.

Rnd 34: (K 4, k 2 tog) 17 times, (k 2 tog) 3 times—88 sts.

Rnds 35-41: Follow graph A for flower motif.

Rnd 42: (K 3, k 2 tog) 16 times, end k 8—72 sts.

Rnd 43: Work butterfly motif as follows: * k 1 pink, k 1 white; rep from * around.

Rnd 44: Work even in white.

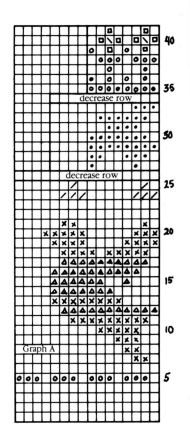

☒ pink
☑ light pink
◉ green
⊡ yellow
⊘ orange
☒ light blue
◮ blue

Earflap Graph

35

Tubular Cord

Tubular cord makes a handsome and stabilizing edge trim for knitted fabrics, and sturdy ties for caps, mitten strings and garment closures. Sometimes called Idiot Cord (or more tactfully, I Cord by Elizabeth Zimmermann) because of what one is reduced to after knitting a few yards of it, tubular cord can be worked on three, four or even more stitches with two double-pointed needles.

Tubular cord. Cast on 3 or 4 sts on a dp needle (depending on how thick you want your cord to be). A Size 3 needle is average for knitting worsted type yarn. *Knit across, slide sts back to right end of same needle, and repeat from *. Instead of casting off at end of cord, thread yarn on blunt needle, pass through sts, and pull up through cord.

Tubular cord edging. Cast 3 sts on a double pointed needle. *K 2, sl 1, pick up and k 1 into edge of fabric, psso. Slide sts to right end of needle, and repeat from *. You can pick up sts along the edge of fabric with a straight or dp needle before you begin the cord, instead of working directly into the fabric.

Sample first for needle size and stitch frequency. This type of edging can draw in if not worked loosely enough.

Rnd 45: * K 1 white, k 1 pink; rep from * around. End off pink.

Rnd 46: With white * k 2, k 2 tog; rep from * around—54 sts.

Rnd 47: Work sun motif as follows: * k 1 gold, k 2 white.

Rnd 48: K 1 white, * k 1 gold, k 2 white; rep from * around to last 2 sts, end k 1 gold, k 1 white.

Rnd 49: * K 2 white, k 1 gold; rep from * around.

Rnds 50-53: Rep Rnds 47, 48, 49, then rep Rnd 47 again. End off white. Continue in gold only.

Rnds 54-55: Work even.

Rnd 56: * K 2, k 2 tog; rep from * around to last 6 sts, end k 6—42 sts.

Rnd 57: * K 1, k 2 tog; rep from * around—28 sts.

Rnd 58: K 2 tog around—14 sts. Thread yarn through sts and fasten off securely.

Right Earflap: Decide at which point you want to position the end of rnd; determine center back if this is different from end of rnd. With Size 3 needles, white yarn, with right side facing and beginning earflap 2½ in (6.5 cm) from center back pick up 15 sts. Using 2 needles, work 7 rows garter st ending with wrong-side row. With right side facing, k 3 then work Row 1 of graph B in st st over center 9 sts, k 3. Keeping 3 sts at each edge in garter st and center 9 sts in st st, continue as established until chart is competed. Work all sts in garter st for 7 rows.

Dec 1 st at beg of each row until 4 sts rem.

Begin tie cord: With 4 rem sts on dpn and working with 2nd dpn, * k 4, slide all sts to right end of needle, pull yarn snugly; with free needle, rep from * until cord is desired length. Break off, thread tail through 4 sts, pull tightly and fasten. Repeat for left earflap.

Cord for lower edge: With wrong side facing and beg at left edge of earflap, * slip lp from each st of cast-on edge to circular needle as far as earflap, then working along outer edge of earflap sl knot from each garter st ridge of earflap to circular needle, skipping sts of tie cord; rep from * around. (Note: Do not pick up and k st in usual way; that would leave a visible ridge on the right side.) Join green to cap and with green cast on 3 sts to dpn. * With 2nd dpn k 2, sl 1, k 1 st from cap, psso cap st; slide 3 sts to right end of dpn, rep from * around entire lower edge of cap.

If you prefer, a crocheted edge and tie cords could be used.

Short Rows Pill Box Cap, *Mary Lamb Becker*

IMAGINE A CAP that fits so comfortably you don't want to take it off—that's Mary Becker's Pill Box. It's knitted sideways in alternate bands of stockinette and reverse stockinette, with short rows for shaping. The garter stitch band is doubled to serve as a casing for elastic, which keeps the hat from stretching out.

All these innovative design features come from lots of experience. Mary, who lives in Milwaukee, Wisconsin, is a freelance knitting pattern editor who has perfected hundreds of designs for *Better Homes and Gardens* and *Vogue Knitting*. She is author of *The Mitten Book*, recently reissued by Dover Books, and served as instruction editor and wise counsel for this book.

For the intermediate knitter.

Size: Adjustable for teen/adult.

Yarn: 1000 yd/lb (2010 m/kg), 12 wraps/in (19/4 cm). Mary used 2 50-g balls of a brushed acrylic yarn, Brunswick Windmist, used double. A single strand of a bulky weight yarn could be substituted.

Miscellaneous materials: Length of elastic, ½ in (12 mm) wide to fit around head comfortably with 2 in (5 cm) overlap. Shrink before using.

Gauge: Over stockinette st with double strand of yarn 3 sts = 1 in (12 sts = 10 cm).

Needles: Single-pointed needles, 16 in (40 cm) long, and one set of dpn, both size 8 (5–5.5 mm, 5) or size to reach gauge given above; tapestry needle.

Instructions: Using invisible cast-on (page 21) and double strand of yarn, cast on 19 sts.

Row 1 (wrong side): Knit.

Row 2: K 17, wrap next st as follows: bring yarn to front of work, sl next st to right needle, bring yarn to back of work, return slipped st to left needle, turn work.

Row 3: Purl 17.

Row 4: K 14, wrap next st, turn.

Row 5: P 14.

Row 6: K 11, wrap next st, turn.

Row 7: Purl 11.

Row 8: Purl 19.

Row 9: Knit 19.

Rep Rows 2–9 fourteen times more. Rep Rows 2–7 once. Slip spare small size double-pointed needle into loops held by cast-on string. Remove string. Rearrange stitches so all are in correct untwisted position (i.e., right half of loop is toward front of needle). Fold cap with right sides together to form tube with needles parallel to each other in a horizontal position, having needle with cast-on edge below needle with last row worked. Yarn is coming from right edge of upper needle. Join edges using kitchener stitch (page 39) and double strand of yarn. Weave in ends.

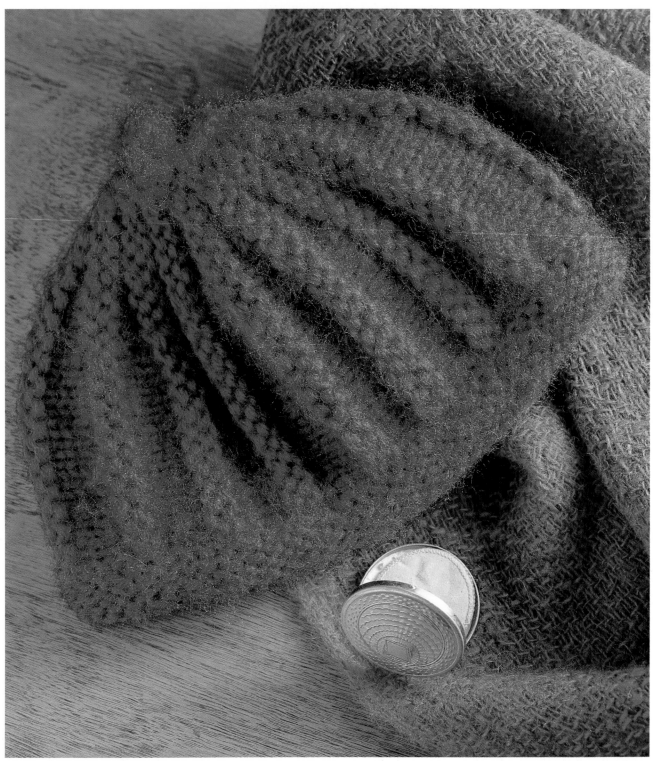

Turn cap right side out. With right side facing, using double strand of yarn and dpn pick up 16 sts around upper edge of cap. Work in reverse st st (purl every rnd) shaping as follows:

Rnd 1: Work even.

Rnd 2: P 2 tog around—8 sts.

Rnd 3: Work even.

Rnd 4: P 2 tog around—4 sts. Work even on rem 4 sts until top nub is as long as desired. Break off, thread yarn through rem sts, pull tight and fasten.

Band: With double strand of yarn and circular needle and with right side facing, pick up 70 sts evenly spaced around lower edge of cap. Turn work so wrong side is facing. K 1 rnd, join and continue to knit around for 5 rnds more. Fit elastic to head with some ease since it will be inserted into headband, overlapping ends; sew ends firmly.

With elastic in place over band and using single strand of yarn, seam sts from needle to selvedge formed when sts were picked up to work band. Leave opening in seam for final adjustment of elastic if needed. If elastic fits comfortably, finish seam; weave in end.

Kitchener Stitch

Where did kitchener stitch get its name? Was there a Mrs. Kitchener? The technique is also called grafting or weaving, and it's a way to join two pieces of knitting invisibly. Butt two sets of stitches, still on their needles, together, right sides up. Thread a strand of matching yarn about four times as long as the join on a blunt, large-eyed needle. Beginning at the right edge, follow this sequence:

1. Bring the yarn needle through the front stitch as if to purl, leaving the stitch on the knitting needle.

2. Bring the yarn needle through the back stitch as if to knit, leaving the stitch on the needle.

3. Bring the yarn needle through the same front stitch as if to knit, and then slip this stitch off the needle. Bring the yarn needle through the next front stitch as if to purl, again leaving the stitch on the needle.

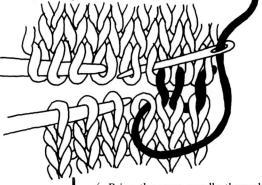

4. Bring the yarn needle through the first back stitch as if to purl, slip that stitch off, and then bring the yarn needle through the next back stitch as if to knit, leaving it on the needle.

Repeat steps 3 and 4 until all stitches have been worked. The yarn needle will enter each stitch twice, once knit-wise and once purl-wise. You can adjust the tension on this row after all stitches have been worked.

Chart

Row numbers (top to bottom): 38, 37, 36, 35, 34, 33, 32, 31, 30, 29, 28, 27, 26, 25, 24, 23, 22, 21, 20, 19, 18, 17, 16, 15, 14, 13, 12, 11, 10, 9, 8, 7, 6, 5, 4, 3, 2, 1

Legend:

- ☐ knit
- ● purl
- Ⓞ yarnover
- ⟋ K 2 tog
- ⟍ ssk
- Ⓐ K 3 tog
- Ⓐ p 3 tog

Lace Double Cap, *Janet Russell*

JANET RUSSELL LOVES all kinds of lace, but lives in Chicago where warm, heavy caps and scarves see more use than airy shawls. When she discovered the Scandinavian *dubbelmossa*, a lined cap usually knitted in color stranded patterns, she quickly saw it as a way to wear lace in the winter.

The cap is two layers thick, with four layers over the ears where the brim turns up. Janet has knitted her name and the date into the lining—no problem checking this hat in the city!

Janet has a full-time career, and spins and knits in her spare time. Her cap similar to this one won the *Spin·Off* magazine handspun cap contest in 1983.

For the intermediate knitter.

Size: Adult medium.

Yarn: 2000 yd/lb (4020 m/kg). Janet used a double strand of unspun Icelandic roving, which comes in a flat wheel. She used a double strand throughout, so her yarn was equivalent to a very soft 1000 yd/lb (2010 m/kg) yarn like Lopi Light. Her source was Meg Swansen (see Resource Guide). The hat requires 2 oz (57 g) of black, 1½ oz (43 g) white, and about 20 yd (18 m) gray.

Gauge: With black yarn worked double over stockinette st 7 sts = 2 in (11 sts = 4 cm).

Needles: Circular needle, 16 in (40 cm) long, and one set of dpn, both size 6 (4-4.5 mm, 7) or size to reach gauge given above; large-eyed yarn needle.

Instructions: Lining: With black wool held double and with dpn cast on 7 sts; join.

Rnd 1: * K 1, inc 1 by making a backward lp on right needle; rep from * around—14 sts.

Rnd 2: Knit.

Rnd 3: * K 2, inc 1 by making backward lp on right needle; rep from * around—21 sts.

Rnd 4: Knit. Continue increasing at seven points every other round until there are 84 sts on needle. Change to circular needle when there are enough sts to reach around needle. Work even in st st for about 3 to 4 in (8-10 cm). Knit name of the recipient into cap at this point following alphabet chart. Knit another 4 rnds after you finish the name for a total of 4 to 5 in (10-12 cm) after the last inc.

Brim: Work turning rnd as follows: K around, wrapping yarn twice around needle for each st. On next rnd let extra turn drop off the needle as each st is knit.

Pattern: Rnd 1: * Sl 1, k 2, pass sl st over 2 knit sts, k 3; rep from * around—70 sts.

Rnd 2: * Yo, k 5; rep from * around—84 sts.

Rnd 3: * K 3, sl 1, k 2, pass sl st over 2 knit sts; rep from * around—70 sts.

Rnd 4: K 3, * yo, k 5; rep from * around to last 2 sts of rnd, end yo, k 2—84 sts.

Rep Rnds 1–4 twice more. Knit another turning rnd. **Brim lining:** With gray yarn, k 2 in (5 cm).

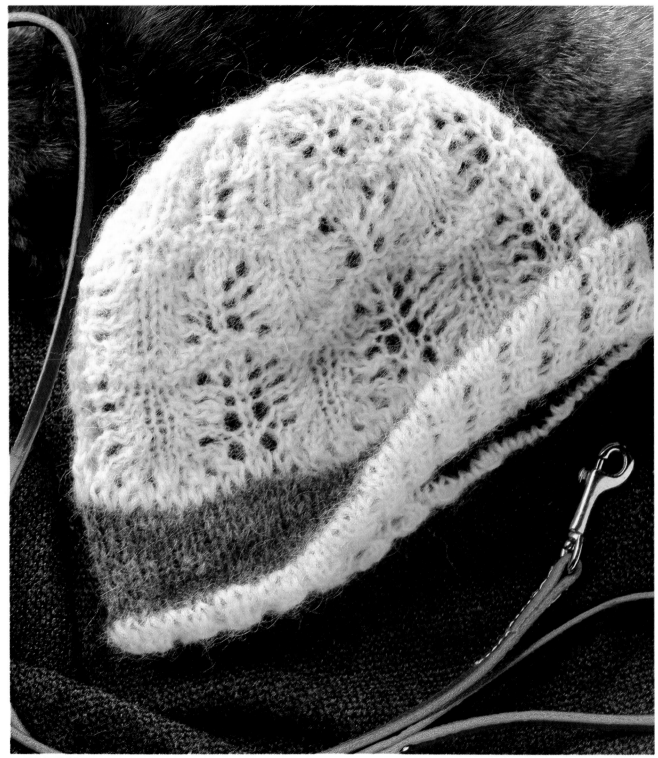

LACE DOUBLE CAP

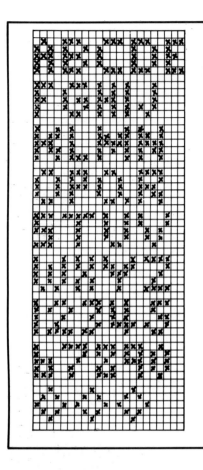

Crown: With white, knit one turning rnd. Using markers, divide the stitches on the needle into 7 groups of 12 sts each. Over each group work the following pattern: (*Note*: Number of sts given at end of dec rnds is number for one section only.)

Rnds 1, 3, 6, 8, 10 and 12: Knit.

Rnds 2 and 4: Purl.

Rnds 5, 7, 9 and 11: K 1, k 2 tog twice, (yo, k 1) 3 times, yo, ssk twice.

Rnds 13-22: Rep Rnds 1-10.

Begin top shaping, changing to dpn when necessary.

Rnd 23: * K 1, k 2 tog twice, yo, k 3, yo, ssk twice—10 sts.

Rnds 24 and 25: Knit.

Rnd 26: Purl.

Rnd 27: K 3 tog, k 7—8 sts.

Rnd 28: Purl.

Rnd 29: K 1, k 2 tog, k 1, (yo, k 1) twice, ssk.

Rnd 30: Knit.

Rnd 31: K 1, k 3 tog, yo, k 1, yo, k 3 tog—6 sts.

Rnd 32: Knit.

Rnd 33: K 1, k 2 tog, yo, k 2, yo, ssk.

Rnd 34: Knit.

Rnd 35: P 3 tog, p 3—4 sts.

Rnd 36: Knit.

Rnd 37: (Yo, k 2 tog) twice.

Rnd 38: Knit.

Rnd 39: K 2 tog around—2 sts.

Rnd 40: Rep Rnd 39—1 st.

Break yarn, thread through the yarn needle, pull strand through single remaining st, and secure end.

Stuff lining inside cap and turn up brim. Or stuff cap inside lining and have a plain black cap with a gray brim.

Lace Watch Cap and Scarf, *Karen Braun*

Since learning to spin ten years ago, Karen Braun has designed most of her own knitwear by necessity—it's often hard to fit handspun yarn to the gauge of a particular pattern. "Spinners all know that a fleece has a life of its own and tells you how it should be spun," Karen notes.

The yarn for this soft lace set was spun from a Corriedale fleece grown by a fellow spinner and sheep raiser in Errington, British Columbia. Karen spun a two-ply yarn about the size of commercial four-ply knitting worsted, and dyed it a subtle gray-blue.

Her source for the classic "Traveling Leaf" pattern was *Traditional Knitting Patterns*, a British book by James Norbury recently reissued by Dover press. Karen added cable edges and borders to the scarf. The cap pattern is written for circular knitting, and the scarf uses the same pattern knitted flat.

Cap for the beginning knitter; scarf, for the intermediate.

Size: Adult; one size fits all.

Yarn: 900 yd/lb (1809 m/kg), 12 wraps/in (19/4 cm). Karen's yarn is a a soft 2-ply handspun Corriedale dyed blue-gray. It's similar in weight to a knitting worsted. The hat requires 3 oz (85 g), and the scarf 6 oz (170 g).

Gauge: Over stockinette st 5 sts = 1 in (8 sts = 4 cm).

Needles: Size 6 (4–4.5 mm, 7) needles or size to reach gauge given above. You'll need 16 in (40 cm) circular and/or a set of dpn for the cap, and straight needles for the scarf.

Cap Instructions: With circular needle, cast on 96 sts. To join, with end of needle with sl knot st in left hand, and being sure sts are not twisted, beg k 2, p 2 rib; insert marker at end of rnd. Continue in k 2, p 2 ribbing as established for 6 in. K 1 rnd, then begin Traveling Leaf pattern:

Rnds 1 and 3: * K 1, yo, k 5, k 2 tog, k 1, k 2 tog through back lp (tbl), k 5, yo; rep from * around.

Rnd 2 and all even-numbered rnds through Rnd 8: Knit.

Rnds 5 and 7: * K 1, k 2 tog tbl, k 5, yo, k 1, yo, k 5, k 2 tog; rep from * around.

Rep Rnds 1–8 once. K 2 rnds.

Begin shaping crown as follows: Rnd 1: * K 10, k 2 tog, place marker; rep from * around—88 sts.

Rnd 2 and all even-numbered rnds through Rnd 22: Knit.

Rnd 3 and all odd-numbered rnds through Rnd 21: * Knit to 2 sts before marker, k 2 tog; rep from * around. At end of Rnd 8, change to dpn; arrange sts as follows: 24 sts on each of first two needles, 16 sts on third needle.

At end of Rnd 22 eight sts rem. Break off, leaving 16 in (40 cm) tail. Thread tail on blunt needle or bodkin and run through rem 8 sts, pull up tightly and fasten off by weaving yarn end in on the inside.

Scarf Instructions: On straight needles, cast on 64 sts.

Border pat: Row 1: Sl 1, k 6, (p 2, k 6) 7 times, p 1.

Row 2 and all even-numbered rows through Row 12: Sl 1, p 6, (k 2, p 6) 7 times, k 1.

Row 3: Rep Row 1.

Row 5: Sl 1, [(sl 3 sts to cable needle and hold in front of work, k 3, k 3 sts from cable needle—cable twist completed), p 2] 7 times, cable twist, p 1.

Rows 7, 9 and 11: Rep Row 1. End of Rnd 12 is end of border pat.

Body of scarf: *(Note:* On Rnds 1, 3, 9 and 11 of body pattern of scarf: Yo at end of last rep of traveling leaf pat must be wrapped around needle before you purl for the beg of the edge pattern.)

Row 1: Sl 1, cable twist, p 1, * k 1, yo, k 5, k 2 tog, k 1, k 2 tog tbl, k 5, yo; rep from * twice, p 1, cable twist, p 1.

Row 2 and all even-numbered rows through Row 16: Sl 1, p 6, k 1, p to last 8 sts, k 1, p 6, k 1.

Row 3: Sl 1, k 6, p 1, * k 1, yo, **k 5,** k 2 tog, k 1, k 2 tog tbl, k 5, yo; rep from * twice, p 1, k 6, p 1.

Row 5: Sl 1, k 6, p 1, * k 1, k 2 tog tbl, **k 5,** yo, k 1, yo, k 5, k 2 tog; rep from * twice, p 1, k 6, p 1.

Row 7: Rep Row 5.

Row 9: Sl 1, k 6, p 1, * k 1, yo, k 5, k 2 tog, k 1, k 2 tog tbl, k 5, yo; rep from * twice, p 1, k 6, p 1.

Row 11: Rep Row 9.

Row 13: Rep row 5.

Row 15: Sl 1, cable twist, p 1, * k 1, k 2 tog tbl, k 5, yo, k 1, yo, k 5, k 2 tog; rep from * twice, p 1, cable twist, p 1.

Rep Rows 9–16 for desired length of scarf, cabling the edge stitches only *every other* Row 15.

Border: Rep Rows 1–11 of Border in reverse order (i.e., Row 11, 10, 9, etc.) Bind off.

Knitting Cables

Cables, according to Priscilla A. Gibson-Roberts in *Knitting in the Old Way*, were used in the earliest embossed knitting, and were adapted by many different cultures. Cables are evident in 18th century Spanish knitting, and have reached their apex in contemporary Aran knitting.

To work a simple cable, move a group of stitches, without working them, from the left needle to a holding needle. Then hold this group *in front* (for a left leaning cable) or *in back* (for a right leaning cable) while working a corresponding number of stitches on the left needle. Then either replace the cable stitches on the left needle and work them, or work them directly off the holding needle, to complete the sequence.

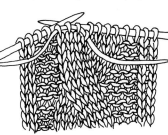

Quick and Easy Balaclava, *Helen Fleischer*

HELEN FLEISCHER of Silver Spring, Maryland, says: "I designed this item in a hurry. My dad's birthday was coming up and I knew he loved my homespun hats, but wanted something that would come down farther to keep his neck and ears warmer.

"I had seen silk balaclavas in a catalog, but had neither the time nor cash to send away for one. Time was running out, so I had to use my wits.

"I cast on as many stitches as I would for a watch cap, then adapted Elizabeth Zimmermann's trick for using ravel yarn to make a face opening. The result was so cozy, I made one for myself, too."

Helen's balaclava is knitted from handspun Corriedale in two shades of natural gray plied together in a yarn size somewhere between sport and knitting worsted weight. She has selected a larger than average needle size so that the fabric has plenty of insulative air space and isn't too confining around the face.

For the beginning knitter.

Size: Adult medium.

Yarn: 900 yd/lb (1809 m/kg), 12 wraps/in (19/4 cm). Helen's yarn is 2-ply handspun Corriedale, one strand each of light and dark gray plied together for a tweedy look. You'll also need a short length of yarn in a contrasting color for the face opening.

Gauge: Over k 1, p 1 ribbing, 5 sts = 1 in (8 sts = 4 cm)

Needles: Circular needle, 16 in (40 cm) length, size 9 (5.5–6 mm, 4) or size to reach gauge given above; circular needle, 16 in (40 cm) length, one size smaller; crochet hook, size H or 8 (5 mm, 6).

Instructions: With larger needle cast on 90 sts using flexible but sturdy edge such as the two-needle cable cast-on method (page 12). Work in k 1, p 1 rib for 60 rnds. With contrast yarn, work 36 sts; sl these 36 sts back to left needle. Continue with original yarn for 1 rnd. Change to smaller needle and work 36 rnds more in rib.

Top shaping: K 2 tog around—45 sts. Knit 3–4 rnds more, then cut yarn, leaving about 12 in (30 cm). Using a tapestry needle, thread yarn through sts, slipping them off the circular needle. Gather tightly, secure end, weave it in.

Face opening: Remove contrast yarn, catching loops on spare needles. Finish face opening with 2 rows of sc, working first row into loops on needles.

A Simple Buttonhole

A three-stitch buttonhole is worked over two rows. On the first row, bind off three stitches in the desired location. On the next row, cast on three stitches over the bound-off ones by making backward loops on the right needle.

This simple method sometimes results in a loose stitch at the beginning of the cast-on. To avoid this, in the second row, increase one in the stitch immediately before the cast-off stitches, and then cast on two additional stitches instead of three.

Ribbed Helmet, *Eleanor Parslow*

ELEANOR PARSLOW of Mt. Solon, Virginia, had been trying for years to come up with a knitted hat that would keep her forehead and ears warm, and be fairly windproof. She found that the stitch for reinforcing stocking heels was just the thing, and the 24-row peak helps protect the sinuses.

"I must confess that this might look better on a child than on a long-nosed, bespectacled, middle-aged lady," she avers.

Eleanor learned to knit in 1940, and to spin in 1983. She spun a softly twisted three-ply from natural gray Hampshire/Suffolk cross for this hat. She's a school librarian and part-time deed researcher for a surveying firm, occasionally a lab technician at James Madison University, and an assistant to her forester husband. She's a lady of many hats!

For the intermediate knitter.

Size: Adult medium.

Yarn: 800 yd/lb (1608 m/kg), 12 wraps/in (19/4 cm). Eleanor used a soft 3-ply handspun Hampshire-Suffolk cross similar in weight to a knitting worsted.

Gauge: Over stockinette st 5 sts = 1 in (8 sts = 4 cm).

Needles: Size 6 (4–4.5 mm, 7) or size to reach gauge given above.

Instructions: Most of this helmet is worked in heel stitch for extra warmth as follows:
  Row 1 (right side): * K 1, sl 1 with yarn in back; rep from * across.
  Row 2: Purl.
Cast on 22 sts. K 2, * p 2, k 2; rep from * across. Continue in k 2, p 2 rib until piece measures 2¼ in (6 cm) ending with a wrong-side row. Break off yarn.

Begin shaping each side of center top section. **Row 1:** With right side of rib section facing and beginning at lower right corner, pick up 10 sts along edge, place marker, beg heel st: (K 1, sl 1 with yarn in back) across, place second marker; working down along opposite side of ribbed section, pick up 10 sts—42 sts.

Row 2 (wrong side): (P 2, k 2) twice, p 2, sl marker, p 22, sl marker, (p 2, k 2) twice, p 2.

Row 3: Work in rib as established to first marker, sl marker, [make a st with backward lp on right needle (M1), sl 1 with yarn in back] twice, continue in heel st to 2 sts before next marker, (k 1, M1) twice, sl marker, rib to end of row—46 sts.

Row 4: Rib to marker, sl marker, p to next marker, sl marker, rib to end of row.

Rep Rows 3 and 4 until there are 42 sts bet markers and 62 sts in all ending with Row 4. Cast on 14 sts at beg of next 2 rows, working sts outside of markers in rib and sts bet markers in heel st—90 sts. Continue in rib and heel st pats until length from cast-on 14 sts is 1¼ in ending with wrong-side row. Work all sts in heel st, working even until piece measures 8 in (20 cm) from cast-on 14 sts. Bind off; fold in half vertically with right sides tog; sew bound off sts with whip st.

Neckband: With right side facing, pick up 72 sts along lower edge; cast on 28 sts for tab. Work k 2, p 2 rib for 5 rows. At end opposite tab, make 3-st buttonhole 4 sts from edge. Continue ribbing for 8 rows more. Bind off. Put button on tab so hood is snug.

RIBBED HELMET

Felted Bonnet, *Vera Tonry*

VERA TONRY of East Moriches, New York, is best known among handspinners for her elegant, fluffy, luxurious dog hair yarns. The green cap here shows another side of Vera's talent—her willingness to play and experiment. Wanting a warm, windproof cap that could be made to fit a variety of head sizes without too much bother with gauge, here's what Vera did:

She found a pattern she liked, made from a fine yarn at 10 sts to the inch in a ribbed stitch. She knitted the pattern using larger yarn and needles and stockinette stitch. This resulted in a giant hat far too large for any human head. Vera tossed it into the washing machine with soap and hot water, then into the dryer, where it shrank and felted down to her size.

"This idea will probably work with any pattern," she says, "so long as you use a 100% wool yarn. Keep in mind that once the hat is felted, it will no longer stretch the way a knitted fabric does. It will behave more like a piece of felt, which it essentially is."

The more the hat is washed and dried, the smaller it will become, up to a point. It would be wise to knit a good size sample swatch, and wash and dry it with periodic checks to see what percentage it has shrunk at different points in the cycle.

For the beginning knitter.

Size: Adult medium. This cap can fit any size, depending on how much you shrink and felt it.

Yarn: 1000 yd/lb (2010 m/kg), 12 wraps/in (19/4 cm). Vera used 3½ oz (100 g) knitting worsted; note that the yarn *must* be 100% wool.

Gauge: Over stockinette st, 7 sts = 2 in (14 sts = 10 cm).

Needles: Circular needle, 16 in (40 cm) length, and single-pointed needles, both size 8 (5–5.5 mm, 6) or size to reach gauge given above; crochet hook, size G or 6 (4.5 mm, 7).

Instructions: Earflap (make 2): Starting at tip of earflap, with single-pointed needles, cast on 12 sts. Working in st st, inc 1 st at beg and end of each knit row until there are 56 sts, ending with a purl row.

Joining rnd: With right side of earflaps facing, knit left earflap to circular needle. Cast on 1 st, place marker on needle, cast on 10 sts, place marker, cast on 1 st, k sts of right earflap to needle, place marker for center back and end of rnd—124 sts. Join by working 1 rnd even.

Shaping: Rnd 1: Sl 1, k 1, psso, k to within 2 sts of marker, k 2 tog, sl marker, k 10, sl marker, sl 1, k 1, psso, work to within last 2 sts of rnd, k 2 tog—120 sts.

Rnd 2 and all even-numbered rnds following: Work even.

Rep Rnds 1 and 2 until 36 sts remain, changing to dpn if necessary. Fold in half at center back and weave rem sts together using kitchener stitch (page 39). Machine wash in hot water and machine dry. Check fit; repeat process if hat is still too large.

FELTED BONNET & GARTER STITCH BONNET

When fit is right, turn back flap at lower front edge about 1½ in (4 cm). With crochet hook work single crochet through both flap and hat, holding flap in place; do not end off, but continue to work 50 ch sts. Turn, sc in 2nd ch from hook and every rem ch. Fasten off. Rep for other side. Steam lightly.

Garter Stitch Bonnet, *Sara Lamb*

THIS LITTLE BONNET is simple enough that a child could make it— really! It would be a marvelous first project for a very young knitter. It can be worked in fine yarns or thick ones, in elaborate patterns or simple garter stitch as shown here, and for large or tiny heads.

It's a simple rectangle, folded back at the front edge and drawn into a gathered back. The cap shown here is sized to fit a four to six year old. Sara chose garter stitch because it's quick and warm. "A friend who was raised abroad," she relates, "told me that as children, their woolen undershirts were knit in garter stitch, not only to hold the garment's shape and give neat edges, but to provide insulating air spaces to trap warmth."

Sara, who lives in Auburn, California, is a weaver, spinner, dyer and knitter of ten years' experience. She teaches and judges all these crafts, and her work has appeared in *Handwoven* and *Spin·Off* magazines. She enjoys teaching handcrafts at the Waldorf School that her two sons attend, and is active in the Sacramento Weavers and Spinners Guild and the Sierra Spinners in Auburn.

For the beginning knitter.

Size: 4- to 6-year-old child.

Yarn: 900 yd/lb (1809 m/kg), 12 wraps/in (19/4 cm). Sara used a 3-ply handspun Lincoln-Corriedale cross wool dyed with indigo. A knitting worsted weight yarn could be substituted.

Gauge: Over garter st 4 sts = 1 in (6 sts = 4 cm).

Needles: One pair, size 9 (5.5–6 mm, 4) or size to reach gauge given above; crochet hook, size G or 6 (4.5 mm, 7) or H or 8 (5 mm, 6).

Instructions: Cast on 44 sts. Knit until piece measures 8 in (20 cm). Without casting off, draw 5 in (13 cm) length of yarn through all sts and pull tightly to draw up the edge. Secure end of yarn by weaving in the end carefully.

Fold back front edge for desired width of cuff. Allowing 10 in (25 cm) tail, work 1 row of single crochet along lower edge of bonnet, working beginning and end of row through both thicknesses of turned back cuff and bonnet. At end of row leave 20 in (50 cm) loop for tie, and work second row of sc. At end of second row end off, leaving 10 in (25 cm) tail.

Make twisted cord ties (page 83).

yarn through last row;
pull up tight to gather

fold back front
edge for cuff

8"

11"

crochet along
bottom edge

Cross Country Ski Hat, *Romedy Murrow*

"THIS HAT IS a mutt evolved from the combined elements of all the ski hats I've ever seen," says Romedy Murrow, Greenland, New Hampshire.

Pattern work is simple because the hat is a straight tube with no shaping at the top. The whole hat, not just the cuff, could be worked in two colors for extra warmth. The hem, turned to show just a little on the outside, is a silky soft yarn (Romedy's special handspun blend of kid mohair, Angora and Finn sheep wool) to cuddle the ears. Truly a hat with hybrid vigor!

For the intermediate knitter.

Size: Adult large.

Yarn: 700 yd/lb (1400 m/kg), 12-14 wraps/in (19-22/cm). Romedy used several different 2- and 3-ply yarns in this hat, all similar in size to a sport yarn. Her yarns tend to be heavy for their diameter because hair fibers like alpaca and llama are heavier than wool. She used 1 oz (28 g) of handspun angora-wool blend for the lining, 3 oz (85 gm) for the main color, and ½ oz (14 g) of each of the three pattern colors in various blends of handspun alpaca, llama, camel down, and wool.

Gauge: Lining: With smaller needles over stockinette st 11 sts = 2 in (9 sts = 4 cm); 8 rows = 1 in (12 rows = 4 cm). Outer layer: With larger needles over stockinette st 5 sts = 1 in (8 sts = 4 cm); 6 rows = 1 in (9 rows = 4 cm).

Needles: Circular needle, 16 in (40 cm) length, size 3 (3.25 mm, 10) and size 4 (3.5 mm, 9) or size to reach gauge given above; single-pointed needles at least 10 in (25 cm) long, in larger size; crochet hook size E or 4 (3.5 mm, 9) or size F or 5 (4 mm, 8).

Instructions: Lining: With smaller circular needle and the lining yarn cast on 105 sts *very loosely*, or cast on to larger circular needle and knit back onto smaller circular needle. Mark the end of the rnd.

Work in k 1, p 1 ribbing for 3 rnds. Change to st st and work for 3½ in (9 cm).

Outer layer: Change to main color and knit sts onto larger needle. Knit 3 rows more, then work chart as follows: Rep from A to B to last 9 sts, then work from A to X. Continue from chart as established; when 13 rows of chart are completed darn ends of pattern colors into back of stitches, continuing with main color only.

Hem: Fold lining up so wrong sides are together and hem covers wrong side of charted design; pin in place. Two or three rows of lining should be visible on the right side. With crochet hook, insert hook as to knit into first stitch on left needle, remove stitch from needle, then insert hook through back loop of first cast-on st. Yo and draw loop through both stitches. Sl loop onto right needle being careful not to twist it. Continue around matching stitch for stitch, being careful not to skip any. Do not work tightly; check that loops being put on right needle are the same tension as previous rows. If done correctly the hem will be invisible on the right side.

Knit to 6½ in (17 cm) from top of the hem, or the desired height, dec 1 st at the end of the last rnd—104 sts. The hat is slightly taller than it is wide.

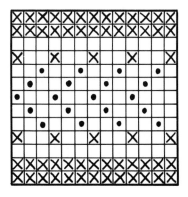

K 15 sts of next rnd. This is so color joins won't be right in the front. Divide the stitches, placing half onto one single-pointed needle (I use 10-in dpn and put rubber stops on the end) and half on the other.

Break yarn, leaving 50–60 in tail. Use kitchener stitch (page 39) to finished top of hat. Do *not* break yarn. Turn hat inside out; fold in half vertically with the two top corners together; with the remaining yarn sew the corners together securely, forming a tapered top. Turn right side out.

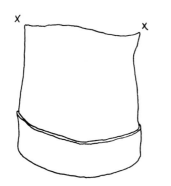

Rainbow Cap and Scarf, *Jean Newsted*

P RECIOUS YARNS ask to be knitted into special projects. Jean Newsted, Calgary, Alberta, spun gossamer fine yarns of silk, wool and angora and dyed them in rainbow hues for this cap and scarf set. One yarn is strands of wool and silk plied together, the other is angora from her own rabbits. The angora dyed a shade lighter than the wool/silk yarn, so she used two rows of each yarn in each four-row pattern repeat for a subtle shaded effect. She knitted the pattern bands in rainbow order and then reversed the colors, giving double-wide stripes of red and purple where the reverses occur. Her aim was a dressy, lacy scarf for her daughter to wear with a white rabbit-fur jacket.

Jean says the most time-consuming part of the project was darning in all the loose ends. "I wouldn't recommend adapting this pattern to a heavier weight yarn, as the darned ends would be too heavy for the lacy pattern," she cautions.

Jean is a spinner, knitter and weaver who teaches knitting at her local yarn store, and spinning for the Red Cross.

For the intermediate knitter.

Size: Adult; one size fits all.

Yarn: 3500-4000 yd/lb (7000-8000 m/kg), 36 wraps/in (28/2 cm). Jean's handspun yarns are a very fine lace weight, but textured enough that they hold their shape in the open stitch she used. One yarn is a 2-ply wool and silk, the other a single-ply

angora. Try substituting a fine brushed mohair for one, a smoother lace yarn for the other, but check your gauge. The set requires about 400 yd (360 m) of yarn in all: 40 yd (36 m) of each yarn style in red, orange, green, blue, and violet.

Gauge: Over pattern st 7 sts = 1 in (11 sts = 4 cm).

Needles: Circular needle, 16 in (40 cm) length, and one set of dpn, both size 7 (4.5–5 mm, 6) or size to reach gauge given above.

Instructions: With red wool and silk cast on 121 sts.

Rnd 1: * (K 2 tog, yo) 4 times, k 3; rep from * around.

Rnd 2: Knit.

Rnds 3 and 4: Change to red angora and knit.

Rep Rnds 1-4 for pat, working Rnds 1 and 2 in wool and silk and Rnds 3 and 4 in angora in the following color sequence: 4 rnds orange/gold, 4 rnds green, 4 rnds blue, 8 rnds purple, 4 rnds blue, 4 rnds green, 4 rnds orange/gold, 8 rnds red, 4 rnds orange/gold.

Ending off: Rnd 1: Work Pat Rnd 1 with green wool and silk.

    Rnd 2: K 3 tog around, end k 1—41 sts.

    Rnd 3: With green angora, knit.

    Rnd 4: K 3 tog around, end k 2—15 sts.

Break off yarn. Thread end through tapestry needle and draw through remaining sts on needle. Make a pompon if desired and attach to top of hat.

Scarf Instructions: Cast on 32 sts loosely in red wool and silk. Work pattern stitch (given below) in the following sequence: Rows 1 and 2 with wool and silk, Rows 3 and 4 with angora. At the same time work pattern in 4 rows of each color in the following color sequence: Red, orange/gold, green, blue, purple; repeat these colors in the reverse order for a total of 40 rows. Rep these 40 rows 5 times more. On the last repeat of the 4 rows of red, work Rows 1 and 2 with angora and Rows 3 and 4 with wool and silk. Cast off loosely. Darn in ends with an embroidery needle.

Pattern stitch: Row 1: K 1, * (k 2 tog, yo) 4 times, k 3; rep from * once, end (yo, k 2 tog) 4 times, k 1.

Rows 2, 3, and 4: Knit.

Star Tam, *Janet Russell*

JANET WRITES, "I 'unvented' this cap in 1981. It has become one of my favorite emergency presents, since I can knit it up quickly and, once the pattern is established, without paying much attention. I usually knit the name of the recipient into the hem of the cap, since this small extra effort is guaranteed to turn him or her into a jelly of gratitude. It is particularly adaptable to odds and ends of yarn."

Janet was inspired by Elizabeth Zimmermann, who pointed out that a classic tam is made by knitting a band, increasing rapidly for the body of the cap, and then knitting straight up without any shaping. The only decreases are in the very center of the crown. The hat gets its distinctive shape during blocking.

Janet has extended the decreases and balanced them with increases in the body of the hat to create the distinctive star motif.

For the intermediate knitter.

Size: Adult medium.

Yarn: 1000 yd/lb (2010 m/kg), 12–14 wraps/in (19–22/4 cm). Janet used 150 yd (137 m) of blue Harrisville 2-ply, and 20 yd (18 m) gray. This yarn is manufactured especially for weaving, so it's not as fluffy as most knitting yarns until it's been washed. (That's why it takes more wraps per inch than many other yarns of similar yardage). You can wash it in hot, soapy water before use, which fluffs it up, or knit with it as is, as Janet has done, and wash your piece after it's finished.

Gauge: 4–5 sts = 1 in (6–8 sts = 4 cm). (Note: Band is held by elastic and is adjustable.)

Needles: Circular needle, 16 in (40 cm) length, and one set of dpn, both size 6 (4–4.5 mm, 7) or size to reach gauge given above.

Notions: Elastic ¾ in (2 cm) wide to fit around head plus 1 in (2½ cm) seam allowance.

Instructions: Band: With blue and circular needle, cast on 80 sts. Join, being careful not to twist sts. K every rnd until piece measures 2 in (5 cm). (Editor's note: For sharp turning edge, k until piece measures 1 in (2.5 cm), purl 1 rnd, k until piece measures 2 in (5 cm).)

Optional design for band: To knit name into hem, k 2 rnds in background color after the cast-on, then work the next five rnds in two-color knitting for the name following alphabet chart on page 42. Remember to work the name upside down and backwards so that it comes out right side up when hem is sewn in place. Then continue to knit until piece measures 2 in (5 cm).

Inc rnd: * Make 1 st (M1) by forming a backward loop on the right needle, k 2; rep from * around—120 sts. **Next rnd:** Work even.

Pattern: Rnd 1: * Work double decrease as follows: Sl 2, k 1, p2sso; k 10, M1, k 1 (mark this stitch), M1, k 10; rep from * around.

    Rnd 2: Knit.

Repeat Rnds 1 and 2 until piece measures 4–5 in (10–13 cm) from the increase row.

STAR TAM & TAM WITH WHEEL PATTERN

A Rainbow Star Tam

Janet describes a happy variation on her Star Tam:

"I make a rainbow hat by measuring off about seven and a half yards each of ten different colors, tying them loosely together in the order I want, and winding them into a ball. When I come to a knot as I am knitting I undo it, leave a tail of the old color and the new color hanging on the back of the work, and continue knitting. After a few rows I can tie the ends together and darn them in. This ball is about right for the body of the cap.

"At the center of the cap, each two rounds of decreases takes about a half yard less than the previous two rounds, but since the amounts are so small, I estimate the width of each remaining stripe as I go so that the center color is the one I want.

"The brim takes about 20 yards, the body of the cap about 85-100 yards (five and a half yards per two rounds), and the decreasing section about 30 yards."

Work 1 rnd in gray, then begin decreasing for crown changing to dpn when necessary. Color changes can be made at random. Odd-numbered rnds are the same as Rnd 1 of previous pattern. Even-numbered rnds have a double decrease without the compensating increase each side of the marked st; this results in 10 sts being dec each rnd.

Rnd 1: * Double dec, k 10, M1, k 1, M1, k 10; rep from * around.

Rnd 2: * Double dec, k 21; rep from * around—110 sts.

Rnd 3: * Double dec, k 9, M1, k 1, M1, k 9; rep from * around.

Rnd 4: * Double dec, k 19; rep from * around—100 sts.

Rnd 5: * Double dec, k 8, M1, k 1, M1, k 8; rep from * around.

Rnd 6: * Double dec, k 17; rep from * around—90 sts.

Rnd 7: * Double dec, k 7, M1, k 1, M1, k 7; rep from * around.

Rnd 8: * Double dec, k 15; rep from * around—80 sts.

Rnd 9: * Double dec, k 6, M1, k 1, M1, k 6; rep from * around.

Rnd 10: * Double dec, k 13; rep from * around—70 sts.

Rnd 11: Change to gray, * double dec, k 5, M1, k 1, M1, k 5; rep from * around.

Rnd 12: * Double dec, k 11; rep from * around—60 sts.

Rnd 13: * Double dec, k 4, M1, k 1, M1, k 4; rep from * around.

Rnd 14: * Double dec, k 9; rep from * around—50 sts.

Rnd 15: * Double dec, k 3, M1, k 1, M1, k 3; rep from * around. At this point the increases are discontinued.

Rnd 16: * Double dec, k 7; rep from * around—40 sts.

Rnd 17: * Double dec, k 5; rep from * around—30 sts.

Rnd 18: * Double dec, k 3; rep from * around—20 sts.

Rnd 19: * Double dec, k 1; rep from * around—10 sts.

Break off yarn and thread the end into the yarn needle. Draw the thread through the remaining sts and fasten off.

Seam the elastic into a circle. Fold the hem in half and hem down over the elastic. Darn in ends. Finish by washing and stretching over a large dinner plate to dry. The dinner plate gives it its shape.

Tam with Wheel Pattern

Priscilla Gibson-Roberts

PRISCILLA GIBSON-ROBERTS of Lakewood, Colorado, is a dedicated spinner and knitter with a love of the old folk arts and a fascination with the people who pursued them. As author of *Knitting in the Old Way*, she's spent many hours perusing old knitting books and examining museum collections.

Priscilla's design inspiration for this piece came from *The Complete Book of Traditional Fair Isle Knitting* by Sheila McGregor. She knitted it as a special gift for her neighbor, "who does so much for me that I wanted to create something special just for her." The tam has a large diameter because the recipient is a large person with long, heavy hair—"I wanted the tam to look dramatic on her," Priscilla says.

For the expert knitter.

Size: Adult medium.

Yarn: 2400 yd/lb (4800 m/kg), 20 wraps/in (31/4 cm). Priscilla's yarn is a 2-ply handspun Corriedale fingering-weight yarn. The hat requires 150 yd (137 m) dark blue, 100 yd (91 m) light blue, 75 yd (68 m) medium blue, and 50 yd (46 m) white.

Gauge: Over stockinette st 13 sts = 2 in (10 sts = 4 cm); 8 rows = 1 in (12 rows = 4 cm).

Needles: Circular needle, 16 in (40 cm) length, and one set of dpn, both size 3 (3.25 mm, 10) or size to reach gauge given above.

Instructions: With circular needle and dark blue, cast on 132 sts. With dark blue and gray, work k 2, p 2 corrugated ribbing (page 62) for 1–1½ in (3–4 cm). Change to st st, inc on first rnd as follows: * K 2, insert left needle from front to back under horizontal thread between st just completed (on right needle) and next st (on left needle); with right needle knit into the back lp, twisting the st—make 1 st completed (M1); rep from * around to last 4 sts, (k 1, M1) 4 times—200 sts.

Follow chart, working in following colors: (Editor's note: Designer intended that color changes of background color be made at random as knitter chooses.)

Rnds 1-9: MC is dark blue, CC is white.

Rnds 10-12: Work in color of your choice.

Rnds 13-14: MC is light blue, CC is dark blue.

Rnds 15-17: Work in color of your choice.

Rnds 18-19: MC is light blue, CC is medium blue.

Rnd 20: MC is light blue, CC is dark blue.

Rnds 21-22: MC is light blue, CC is medium blue.

Rnds 23 and 24: Light blue.

Rnd 25: MC is dark blue, CC is light blue.

Rnd 26: Dark blue.

Rnds 27-33: MC is dark blue, CC is white.

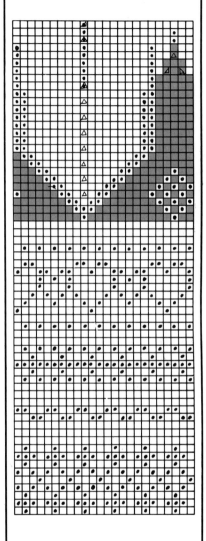

🔺 double decrease

🔻 K 2 tog

◿ ssk

Corrugated Ribbing

Two-color ribbing is decorative and firmer than regular ribbing. While you wouldn't want to use it for a watch cap or other style that molds down around the head, it's most suitable for the band of a well fitting tam.

Use a firm cast-on technique such as the two-needle cable cast-on on page 12. Work one round of k 2, p 2 ribbing in your main color, and then join a contrasting color. As you work subsequent rounds, make all knit stitches in one color, and all purl stitches in the other.

This ribbing will go quickly if you hold the knit color over your left finger and the purl over your right. It's best worked in the round, and most attractive worked as k 2, p 2 ribbing rather than k 1, p 1.

Rnd 34: Dark blue.

Rnd 35: MC is dark blue, CC is light blue.

Rnds 36-37: Light blue.

Next rnd: Continuing with light blue, (k 14, k 2 tog, k 9, place marker) 8 times—192 sts (24 sts in each of 8 sections).

Begin wheel pat, working CC with dark blue throughout and changing MC and working shaping as follows: (Note: Repeat directions below for each of 8 sections. Number of sts at end of dec rows refers to sts in 1 section.)

Rnds 39-45: Work using light blue for MC.

Rnd 39: 2 MC, 1 CC, 11 MC, 1 CC, 9 MC.

Rnd 40: (1 MC, 1 CC) twice, 9 MC, 3 CC, 8 MC.

Rnd 41: (1 CC, 1 MC) twice, 1 CC, 7 MC, 2 CC, 1 MC, 2 CC, 7 MC.

Rnd 42: (1 MC, 1 CC) 3 times, 5 MC, 2 CC, with MC (sl 2, k 1, p2sso), 2 CC, 5 MC, 1 CC—22 sts.

Rnd 43: (1 CC, 1 MC) twice, 1 CC, 5 MC, 2 CC, 3 MC, 2 CC, 5 MC.

Rnd 44: (1 MC, 1 CC) twice, 5 MC, 2 CC, with MC (k 1, sl 2, k 1, p2sso, k 1), 2 CC, 4 MC—20 sts.

Rnd 45: 2 MC, 1 CC, (5 MC, 2 CC) twice, 3 MC.

Rnds 46-49: Work using medium blue for MC.

Rnd 46: 7 MC, 2 CC, with MC (k 2, sl 2, k 1, p2sso, k 2), 2 CC, 2 MC—18 sts.

Rnd 47: 6 MC, 2 CC, 7 MC, 2 CC, 1 MC.

Rnd 48: 5 MC, 2 CC, with MC (k 3, sl 2, k 1, p2sso, k 3), 2 CC—16 sts.

Rnd 49: 5 MC, 2 CC, 7 MC, 2 CC.

Rnds 50–56: Use light blue for MC.

Rnd 50: 5 MC, 2 CC, with MC (k 2, sl 2, k 1, p2sso, k 2), 2 CC—14 sts.

Rnd 51: (5 MC, 2 CC) twice.

Rnd 52: 5 MC, 2 CC, with MC (k 1, sl 2, k 1, p2sso, k 1), 2 CC—12 sts.

Rnd 53: 5 MC, 2 CC, 3 MC, 2 CC.

Rnd 54: 5 MC, 2 CC, with MC (sl 2, k 1, p2sso), 2 CC—10 sts.

Rnd 55: 5 MC, 2 CC, 1 MC, 2 CC.

Rnd 56: 5 MC, with CC (k 1, sl 2, k 1, p2sso, k 1)—8 sts.

Rnds 57-61: Use white for MC.

Rnd 57: 5 MC, 3 CC.

Rnd 58: With MC (ssk, k 1, k 2 tog), 3 CC—6 sts.

Rnd 59: 3 MC, 3 CC.

Rnd 60: With MC (sl 2, k 1, p2sso), 3 CC—4 sts.

Rnd 61: 1 MC, 3 CC. Break off MC. Complete tam with CC.

Rnd 62: K 1, sl 2, k 1, p2sso—2 sts.

Rnd 63: Work even.

Rnd 64: K 2 tog—1 st.

Break off yarn leaving sufficient length to double it over and lace it through the remaining sts. Draw the sts together firmly, working the end in to secure it. Work all remaining ends in.

Lightly steam to block and flatten the top of the tam. To maintain its flat, circular shape, keep the tam blocked over a cardboard circle or plate when not in use.

General Dimensions for a Tam

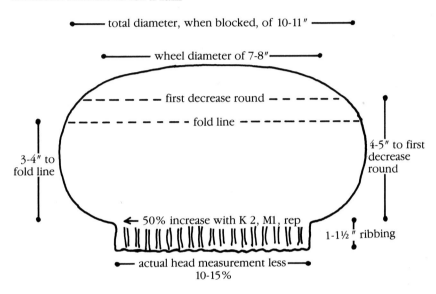

total diameter, when blocked, of 10-11″

wheel diameter of 7-8″

first decrease round

fold line

3-4″ to fold line

4-5″ to first decrease round

← 50% increase with K 2, M1, rep

1-1½″ ribbing

actual head measurement less 10-15%

Garter Stitch Cap and Mittens, *Sue Jones*

S UE JONES of Islesford, Maine, likes to spin local fleece into bulky yarn. She sells her yarns and knitware in a craft co-op in Bar Harbor, and wanted a product that was fast and easy to make, yet would protect against the bitter cold of Maine winters. "To the best of my knowledge," she says, "this cap pattern isn't in any pattern book but that seems impossible since it's so easy." The mittens followed, as she tried to come up with a style that would match the cap better than traditional stockinette stitch ones would.

"The hat really looks a little dull just sitting there," Sue says, "but it's one of those styles that seems to mold to the wearer and flatter her. The hat can be made more colorful and use up scraps of yarn by knitting several rows in contrasting colors, or by knitting up three inches using the main color and then adding a wide band of a contrasting color. I've just completed a stunning one in black with a band of white mohair."

With large needles and only two and a half stitches to the inch, this set knits up quickly and easily—a great project for the beginner or the impatient!

For the beginning knitter.

Size: Adult medium.

Yarn: 300 yd/lb (600 m/kg), 8 wraps/in (12/4 cm). Sue has used 6 oz (170 g) bulky weight irregular handspun in natural white for the cap, and 6 oz (170 g) for the mittens.

Gauge: For cap, over garter st, 4½ sts = 2 in (3½ sts = 4 cm). For mittens, over garter st, 5 sts = 2 in (4 sts = 4 cm).

Needles: For cap, circular needle 16 in (40 cm) length, and one set of dpn, both size 11 (7–7.5 mm, 1) or size to reach gauge given above. For mittens, one set of dpn, size 10 (6–6.5 mm, 3) or size to reach gauge given above; one set of dpn a size smaller.

Cap Instructions: With circular needle cast on 48 sts. Being sure sts are not twisted, begin garter st (k 1 rnd, p 1 rnd), working even until work measures 9 in (23 cm), ending with a p rnd.

Top shaping: Note: Change to dpn as number of sts rem requires.

Rnd 1: (K 4, k 2 tog, place marker) 8 times—40 sts.

Rnd 2 and all even-numbered rnds through Rnd 6: Purl.

Rnds 3 and 5: (K to 2 sts before marker, k 2 tog) 8 times—24 sts at end of Rnd 5.

Rnd 7: K 2 tog around—12 sts.

Break yarn and pull through rem sts, weave tail in.

Mitten Instructions: With smaller needles cast on 24 sts. Divide sts evenly on 3 needles and join, being sure sts are not twisted. Work in k 1, p 1 rib for 3 in (8 cm). Change to larger needles and work in garter st (k 1 rnd, p 1 rnd) for 1 in (2.5 cm) or desired length for thumb opening, ending with a purl rnd.

Thumb opening: Rnd 1: K 7 sts, sl last 5 sts worked to holder for thumb; complete rnd.

Rnd 2: Purl, casting on 5 sts over 5 sts on holder for thumb.

Continue in garter st until length from thumb opening is 5 ½ in (14 cm) or mitten is 1 in (2.5 cm) less than length of hand, ending with a purl rnd.

Finger tip shaping: Rnd 1: * K 2, k 2 tog; rep from * around—18 sts.

Rnd 2: Purl.

Rnd 3: * K 1, k 2 tog; rep from * around—12 sts.;

Rnd 4: Purl.

Rnd 5: K 2 tog around—6 sts.

Break yarn and pull through rem sts; weave in tail.

Thumb: With smaller needles sl 5 thumb sts from holder to needle, pick up 1 st at side of thumb opening, pick up 5 sts along top of thumb opening, pick up 1 st at other side of thumb opening—12 sts. Work in garter st until length of thumb is 2 ½ in (6 cm), ending with a purl rnd.

Thumb shaping: Rnd 1: (K 1, k 2 tog) around—8 sts.

Rnd 2: Purl.

Rnd 3: K 2 tog around—4 sts.

Break yarn and pull through rem sts. Weave in tail.

Work second mitten, reversing position of thumb opening.

Mushroom Cap and Mittens, *Jacqueline Fee*

W HEN JACQUELINE FEE's book, *The Sweater Workshop,* hit the bookstores four years ago, her Mushroom Cap pattern quickly became a favorite of knitters everywhere because it was simple to knit using any yarn, and because it did its job so well. The theory behind the cap is simplicity itself:

—Knit a gauge swatch in stockinette stitch with whatever yarn on whatever needles to determine stitches per inch.

—Measure your head diameter and multiply times stitches per inch to get the cast-on number.

—Work ribbing for three inches or so.

—Work the crown in stockinette stitch.

—Work decrease rounds for a couple of inches, and end off.

This approach to cap knitting is extremely freeing, and can be applied to many other basic patterns. An interesting and useful general fact that Jackie notes is this: "The cap's crown depth is equal to the length of an adult hand. Therefore, the same stripe sequence will fit into your favorite mitten pattern. Actually, one mitten is half a cap, or conversely, a cap is two mittens—a fact that might help you figure yarn amounts in any situation."

The Mushroom Cap variation shown here uses stripes and a few rows of alternating dark-light stitches for a lively pattern that's simpler than it looks. Neither color is unused for more than a couple of rounds, so they can be carried up to eliminate darning in loose ends. The crown is decreased down to only three stitches, which are then worked as a tubular cord (see page 36), and finished off with a tassle. The mittens are a classic accompaniment.

Jackie lives in Hingham, Massachusetts, where she maintains a knitting mail order business and newsletter.

For the beginning knitter.

Size: Adult medium.

Yarn: 1000 yd/lb (2010 m/kg), 12 wraps/in (19/4 cm). Jackie's yarn is a 2-ply Harrisville wool, washed before using. See yarn notes on the Star Tam (page 58). She used 2 oz (57 gm) each of Denim blue and Oatmeal gray for the cap, and the same amount for the mittens.

Gauge: Over stockinette st 5 sts = 1 in (8 sts = 4 cm).

Needles: For cap, circular needle, 16 in (40 cm) long, size 4 (3.5 mm, 9) or size to reach gauge given above. For mittens, one set of dpn, size 4 (3.5 mm, 9) or size to reach gauge given above.

Cap Instructions: With circular needle and Denim cast on 96 sts. Work k 2, p 2 ribbing for 3 in (8 cm). Place marker at "seamline" (end of rnd) and work following stripe sequence in st st for the crown:

Carrying two colors of yarn in the same row, whether you knit American style (holding yarn in right hand) or Continental style (holding yarn in left hand), can result in a massive tangle that must be untwisted frequently. Learn to hold a yarn in *each* hand, and your two-color knitting will proceed smoothly and quickly. Jackie Fee's patterned Mushroom Cap is an ideal project for practicing what might at first seem like an awkward technique.

Rnd	c1	c2	c3	c4
20	X		X	
19	X	X	X	X
18	X	X	X	X
17				
16				
15	X		X	
14				
13				
12	X	X	X	X
11	X		X	
10	X	X	X	X
9				
8	X		X	
7				
6	X	X	X	X
5	X	X	X	X
4				
3				
2	X	X	X	X
1				

☐ = Oatmeal

☒ = Denim

Color pattern sequence: Rnd 1: Oatmeal. **Rnd 2:** Denim. **Rnds 3 and 4:** Oatmeal. **Rnds 5 and 6:** Denim. **Rnd 7:** Oatmeal. **Rnd 8:** * K 1 Denim, k 1 Oatmeal; rep from * around. **Rnd 9:** Oatmeal. **Rnd 10:** Denim. **Rnd 11:** Rep Row 8. **Rnd 12:** Denim. **Rnds 13 and 14:** Oatmeal. **Rnd 15:** Rep Rnd 8. **Rnds 16 and 17:** Oatmeal. **Rnds 18 and 19:** Denim. **Rnd 20:** Rep Rnd 8. **Rnds 21–39:** Work Rnds 1–19 in reverse order (i.e., Rnd 19, 18, 17, etc.) Work 1 rnd of Denim, then beg crown dec.

Crown decrease: Rnd 1: (K 6, k 2 tog) around.

Rnd 2 and all even-numbered rnds through Rnd 12: Knit.

Rnd 3: (K 5, k 2 tog) around.

Rnd 5: (K 4, k 2 tog) around. Change to dpn.

Rnd 7: (K 3, k 2 tog) around.

Rnd 9: (K 2, k 2 tog) around.

Rnd 11: (K 2 tog) around.

Rnd 13: (K 2 tog) around.

Rnds 14 and 15: Rep Rnd 13—3 sts rem.

Put these 3 sts on one dpn. With a second dpn, work knitted cord for desired length as follows: * K 3, do not turn work, slide 3 sts to other end of needle, put empty needle in right hand, rep from *. Attach tassel of two colors.

Mitten Instructions: Right mitten: With Denim cast on 44 sts. Divide on 3 needles (12, 16, 16) being careful not to twist. Work at least 3 in (8 cm) of k 2, p 2 rib. Change to st st and work first 6 rnds only of the color pattern sequence (given above).

At the same time when Rnd 6 is completed, begin thumb gusset as follows:

Thumb gusset: Rnd 7: K 2, place marker, inc in next st, k 2, inc in next st, place marker, work to end of rnd—46 sts.

Rnd 8: Work even.

Rnd 9: K 2, sl marker, inc in next st, k 4, inc in next st, sl marker, work to end of rnd—48 sts.

Rnd 10: Work even.

Rnds 11–17: Continue inc in st after first marker and st before 2nd marker every other rnd—16 sts bet markers (56 sts in all).

Rnd 18: K 2, sl 16 thumb sts to holder, cast on 4 sts, join and work to end of rnd—44 sts.

Work even through Rnd 39 completing the color sequence, then break Oatmeal and work tip decs with Denim as follows:

Tip decs: Rnd 1: (K 3, k 2 tog) 8 times, end k 2, k 2 tog—35 sts.

Rnds 2, 3 and 4: Work even.

Rnd 5: (K 2, k 2 tog) 8 times, end k 3—27 sts.

Rnds 6 and 7: Work even.

Rnd 8: (K 2, k 2 tog) 6 times, end k 3—21 sts.

Rnd 9: Work even.

Rnd 10: (K 1, k 2 tog) 7 times—14 sts.

Rnd 11: Work even.

Rnd 12: K 2 tog around—7 sts.

Fasten off by breaking the yarn and drawing the end through the rem sts and secure.

Thumb: Continue in color sequence as established, working as follows: Divide the 16 thumb sts on 2 needles. With third needle, pick up and k 4 sts around opening of thumb, complete rnd—20 sts.

Work even for 1½ in, then break Oatmeal and work tip decs as follows:

Tip decs: Rnd 1: (K 3, k 2 tog) around—16 sts.

Rnds 2, 4 and 6: Work even.

Rnd 3: (K 2, k 2 tog) around—12 sts.

Rnd 5: (K 1, k 2 tog) around—8 sts.

Rnd 7: K 2 tog 4 times, then fasten off by breaking the yarn and drawing it through the rem 4 sts and secure.

Left mitten: Work as the right one to the beg of thumb gusset, then:

Rnd 7: K 24, place marker, inc in next st, k 2, inc in next st, place marker, work to end of rnd.

Rnd 8: Work even.

Rnd 9: K 24, sl marker, inc in next st, k 4, inc in next st, sl marker, work to end of rnd. Work the rem of the mitten as for the right one.

Two-End Cap and Gauntlet Mittens
Meg Swansen

MANY KNITTERS credit their mother or grandmother with teaching them the craft. Meg Swansen of Pittsville, Wisconsin, received a rich education from her own mother, Elizabeth Zimmermann, and has gone on to join her in a knitting business that includes a semiannual newsletter, mail order tools and supplies, and summer "knitting camps" that have inspired and educated countless knitters over the years.

Living near each other in rural Wisconsin, Meg and Elizabeth have ample opportunity to share ideas and urge each other on. Their work takes on a creative resonance as they bounce ideas back and forth. Take, for example, this "Two-End" knitted set. The idea of knitting off both ends of a ball of yarn is an old one, dating back to early Scandinavian knitting. It

TWO-END CAP & GAUNTLET MITTENS

Casting On For Two-End Knitting

The object is to have single cast-on loops on your needle, but a double strand of yarn to work from. The simplest way to achieve this to cast on in the usual way, and then join the second strand before beginning to knit.

Meg Swansen's technique is to use the One Needle Cast-on (page 12), holding both strands coming from the ball over the thumb but a single strand of "tail" over the index finger. This gives a sturdy doubled edge, and a couple of loose ends to darn in.

Priscilla A. Gibson-Roberts, on the other hand, casts on using each of the two ends alternately, bringing each end up under the previous one as cast-on loops are made. This technique would be particularly appropriate if you were knitting with two different colors instead of two ends from the same ball.

Lizbeth Upitis' two strand cast-on (page 114) also uses the One Needle Cast-on, but with two yarn colors; one forms a decorative edge.

was virtually lost for years, but has been revived through Elizabeth's *Wool Gathering* newsletter and Priscilla A. Gibson-Roberts' *Knitting in the Old Way*. Meg has pushed its decorative potential, and incorporated a clever and unique "curled tip" finger decrease that her mother invented, or "unvented", back in 1966. See Carol Rhoades' Two-End Mittens on page 113 for a very different application of this technique.

For the expert knitter.

Size: Adult average.

Yarn: 840 yd/lb (1688 m/kg), 12 wraps/in (19/4 cm). Meg has used 2-ply Sheepswool which she sells by mail order (see Resource Guide). The hat requires 4 oz (113 g) of natural white, and the mittens another 4 oz (113 g) plus 2 oz (57 gm) light gray.

Gauge: Over stockinette st, 5 sts = 1 in (8 sts = 4 cm).

Needles: Circular needle 16 in (40 cm) length, and one set of dpn, both size 5 (3.75–4 mm, 8) or size 6 (4–4.5 mm, 7) or size to reach gauge given above.

A note about the technique: Two-end knitting is so called because you knit from both ends of the same ball of wool. Let's call the two ends strand A and strand B. While authentic Scandinavian two-end knitting requires carrying both threads over the right finger and twisting them between each stitch, you can get similar pattern effects (though not the same firm fabric) by holding the yarn as for two-color knitting with one strand in each hand (see page 68), or any other way that allows you to work alternately from strands A and B. When working on an even number of sts as in this cap, each rnd begins with one strand and ends with the other. Since every rnd should begin with the opposite strand as the previous rnd, this means the last st of a rnd and the first st of the following rnd are worked with the same strand. However, since both strands are the same color, beginning a rnd with the opposite strand as the previous rnd is *not* a critical factor and won't make a visible difference.

To illustrate how the technique works, let Meg talk you through the first two rnds of the chart shown opposite. The circles represent purl sts made with B in front, and loops represent knit sts made with B in front and A in back. The blank squares are k sts, worked alternately with A and B.

Begin with Rnd 9 at bottom right corner of the graph. Strand A is in back, strand B is in front.

Rnd 9: * P 1 B, k 1 A, p 1 B, take B to back, k 1 A, k 1 B, k 1 A, take B to front, p 1 B, k 1 A, p 1 B, take B to back, k 1 A, k 1 B, k 1 A; rep from * around.

Rnd 10: * With A in back and B in front, k 1 A, p 1 B, k 1 A, take B to back, k 1 B, k 1 A, take B to front, p 1 B, k 1 A, p 1 B, k 1 A, p 1 B, take B to back, k 1 A, k 1 B; rep from * around. Now try the cap.

Cap Instructions: Cast on 84 sts, join. Join in a second strand of the same wool. (Or use one of the two-end cast-ons described at left.)

Rnd 1: * With strand B in back k 1, with strand A in front p 1; rep from * around.

Rnd 2: With both strands in back, k around, alternating strands. This is referred to as a plain rnd.

Rnd 3: Rep Rnd 1.

Rnd 4: With both strands in front, p around, alternating strands.

Rnds 5 and 6: Rep Rnd 2 (plain rnds).

Rnd 7: With both strands in front, p around alternating strands, but take each "new" strand from under the "old" strand. Yes, this will twist the wools around each other in a bit of a tangle, but it is only 1 rnd and see how handsome it is!

Rnd 8: Rep Rnd 2 (plain rnd).

Rnds 9–19: Work from chart.

Rnd 20: Rep Rnd 2 (plain rnd).

Rnd 21: Rep Rnd 4.

Rnds 22 and 23: Rep Rnd 2 (plain rnd).

Rnds 24, 26, 28 and 30: Rep Rnd 1.

Rnds 25, 27 and 29: Rep Rnd 2 (plain rnd).

After Rnd 30, continue with both strands in back, k all sts, alternating strands. If you are tired of working alternate strands, you can shift back to 1 strand for the rest of the cap. In either case, knit another 10–15 rnds in plain st. Work a 7 point top dec: * K 9, *sl 2 tog knitwise, k 1, p2sso—double dec completed*, rep from * around 70 sts. Knit 1 rnd plain. Now work double dec every rnd (changing to 4 dpn when necessary): * K 7, double dec; rep from * around, etc., down to 14 sts. K 2 tog around—7 sts.

Run wool through sts and finish off. (Tassel optional.)

Mitten Instructions: With CC (gray) cast on 60 sts; join second strand.

Rnds 1 and 2: With both strands in front of work, p around, alternating strands.

Rnd 3: With both strands in back, k around, alternating strands.

Rnd 4: With B in front and A in back, (p 1 B, k 1 A) around.

Rnds 5 and 6: Rep Rnd 3.

Rnd 7: Rep Rnd 1.

Rnds 8, 9 and 10: Rep Rnd 3.

Break off 1 strand CC, join 1 strand MC (white).

Rnd 11: With both strands in front, p around alternating strands, always picking up the new strand from *under* the old.

Rnd 12: Rep Rnd 11 but always take new strand *over* the old.

Break off CC, join 2nd strand of MC (white).

Rnd 13: Rep Rnd 3.

Rnds 14–24: Work from graph (Rnds 9–19) for matching hat.

Rnds 25 and 26: Rep Rnd 3.

Rnd 27: Rep Rnd 1.

Rnds 28 and 29: Rep Rnd 3.

Rnds 30 and 31: Rep Rnd 4.

Rnd 32: With both strands in back, (k 1 B, k 2 tog with A) around—40 sts.

Rnd 33: Rep Rnd 3.

Rnd 34: Rep Rnd 4.

diamond

purl-chain

 knit st with strand A; B is held in front

 purl st with strand B; A is held behind

with both strands behind, K with alternate strands

Now, the rest of the mitten is worked in st st with both strands in back using alternate strands as in Rnd 3. You may interject texture wherever you like, since you always have both strands at your disposal. The pair shown here has just a bit each side of the thumb.

K 1 in (2.5 cm) for wrist. Mark 3 sts at beg for thumb gusset. Work an inc each side of those 3 sts every 2nd rnd until you have a total of 19 sts. A sneaky way to increase: the row *before* the inc, work 1 st with both strands; next rnd, knit into each of those strands separately! Put the 19 sts on a thread. Cast on (by backward loops) 3 sts in their place and continue around until mitten is the height of the top of your little finger.

Choose center back stitch—now this is when you get to decide just where you want the thumb to be placed on the mitten. You've seen those Norwegian mittens where the thumb lies flat on the palm; other mittens have the thumb coming out at a right angle from the hand; Meg puts her thumb somewhere in between.

So, mark the center back stitch and work a double dec (sl 2 tog knitwise, k 1, pass 2 slipped sts over) there every other rnd for 3 rnds then every rnd until you have half the number of hand sts you began with. You will now be on dpn. Weave the remaining sts from the dec to the tip. Try it on—you will see how it feels like an old friend already—and even without a thumb.

Tapered thumb: On dpn pick up the 19 sts, plus the 3 cast-on sts. Knit around, working that double dec up the inside of the thumb every 2nd rnd, causing it to taper elegantly. Draw a thread through the remaining 11 sts and pull them up tightly. Finish off ends and block.

Optional simple thumb: Knit straight to wanted length; k 2 tog around, end k 1—10 sts. Draw yarn through rem sts, pull and fasten tightly.

Fluffy Cap and Mitten Set, *Ingvor Johnson*

KNITTING A flat tube on only two needles is a marvelous trick that's been used in a number of patterns in this book. Ingvor Johnson learned it years ago from an elderly friend in her native Sweden, and has used it to make a double layer fabric for these elegant angora-blend mittens for her daughter. It would be equally suitable for the hat, although she's chosen to knit it in one long tube with the lining half stuffed up into the patterned outside half.

For the main color, Ingvor has blended together angora and fine wool and spun a soft two-ply yarn. The blue pattern yarn in the cap has a little silk blended in as well, and is dyed with indigo. Ingvor and her lucky daughter live in Setauket, New York.

For the beginning knitter.

Size: Adult average.

Yarn: 2200 yd/kb (4422 m/kg), 18 wraps/in (28/4 cm). Ingvor's main color yarn is a soft, fuzzy 2-ply blend of 60% angora and 40% wool. The blue pattern yarn in the cap is angora, indigo-dyed silk and wool blended together. She used 5 oz (142 g) MC

FLUFFY CAP & MITTEN SET

for the hat and 3 oz (85 g) for the mittens, and ½ oz (14 g) CC for the hat. If you substitute a less fluffy yarn, choose one that's heavier—perhaps a sport weight. And check your gauge.

Gauge: Over stockinette st, 11 sts = 2 in (9 sts = 4 cm).

Needles: Circular needle, 16 in (40 cm) length, and one set of dpn, both size 2 (2.75–3 mm, 11) or size 3 (3.25 mm, 10) or size to reach gauge given above.

Cap Instructions: This is a double layer hat. Beginning at the top of the inner layer, with dpn and MC cast on 6 sts.

Rnd 1: Inc in each st around—12 sts.

Rnd 2: * K 1, inc in next st; rep from * around—18 sts.

Rnd 3: Work even. Continue increasing every other rnd with 1 more st in between incs until you have 108 sts. Change to circular needle and work even until length is 21 in (53 cm) from the beginning. Work 21 rnds from chart, repeating as needed around hat. When chart is completed, begin decs as follows:

Decrease: Rnd 1: (K 16, k 2 tog) around—102 sts.

Rnd 2: Work even.

Rnd 3: (K 15, k 2 tog) around—96 sts.

Rnd 4: Work even.

Continue to dec 6 sts every other rnd until 6 sts rem. Draw yarn through and fasten. Tuck lining half inside patterned half.

Mitten Instructions: With single-pointed needles cast on 80 sts. Knit on 2 needles for 4 in (10 cm) in double knit (dk) as follows: **Double knit:** * K 1, with yarn in front of st (wyif) sl 1 as to purl; rep from * across. Rep this row until work measures 4 in (10 cm).

Mark for thumb: To mark the front side: Work 40 sts in dk, with contrasting color work next 18 sts in dk, sl these last 18 sts back to left needle and with main color work the 18 sts again, then complete the last 22 sts in dk.

Next row: To mark the back side: Work 22 sts in dk, work 18 sts with contrasting color in dk, sl these last 18 sts back to left needle, work again in dk with main color; complete row in dk. Continue to work in dk until total length of work measures 8½ in (22 cm), placing a marker in the center of the last row.

Finger tip shaping: On the next 2 rows dec 1 st at the beginning of the row, before and after the marker and at the end of the row by knitting 2 *knit* sts tog as follows: [Insert right needle through 2 k sts as to k 2 tog being sure not to catch the p st between them and k those 2 sts tog, but do not remove them from left needle. Bring yarn forward and below purl st (now buried between the 2 knit sts), and with tip of right needle dig out the purl st and sl it to right needle, allowing 2 sts knit together to sl off left needle (1 k st dec)]. Continue in dk to 4 sts before marker. Rep bet [ ]'s, then with yarn in front sl next p st, sl marker, rep bet [ ]'s, continue in dk pat to last 4 sts, rep bet [ ]'s; with yarn in front, sl last p st—76 sts.

On next dec row, notice that there are 2 k sts together without a p st bet. These are k tog in the usual way as follows: Second dec row: K 2 *knit* sts tog, work in dk to 3 sts before marker, k 2 *knit* sts tog, with yarn in front, sl p st, sl marker, k 2 *knit* sts tog, continue in dk to last 3 sts in row, k 2 *knit* sts tog, wyif sl 1—72 sts.

Work 2 rows in dk without dec. Rep these last 4 rows 4 times more—40 sts. With right side facing, pull yarn through k sts, slipping p sts to spare needle as you come to them; then sl yarn through p sts. Pull tightly and fasten.

Thumb: * Pull out contrasting color yarn on one side of work. This releases 9 lps below opening and 8 lps above. With first dpn pick up 1 st at right corner of opening, sl 9 lps below opening to left needle and k them with first dpn. With 2nd dpn pick up 2 sts at left corner of opening, sl 4 lps above opening to left needle and k them with 2nd dpn. With 3rd dpn, work last 4 lps from above opening—20 sts on 3 dpn. With tapestry needle and smooth twine or perle cotton, sl all sts from needles to thread. Rep from * on opposite side of work. Sl sts to dpn alternating as follows: st from front layer, st from back layer, etc., and dividing sts on 3 dpn—40 sts. Work dk in rnds as follows:

Rnd 1: (K 1, wyif sl 1 as to purl) around.

Rnd 2: (With yarn in back sl 1 as to purl, p 1) around.

Hint: When knitting thumb in dk on dpn in the rnd, it helps to think about a front and a back layer. You must work around the needles twice (one rnd to work the front layer of sts and one rnd to work the back layer) to complete 1 rnd of sts of both layers. When knitting the front layer, you push the back layer aside (by slipping those sts) and the reverse on the following rnd when knitting the back layer.

Continue in this pat until thumb measures 2¾ in (7 cm), then begin dec.

Thumb shaping: K 2 *knit* sts tog on next rnd as follows:

Rnd 1: * Rep bet [ ]'s of finger tip shaping, wyif sl 1; rep from * around—30 sts.

Rnd 2: * Wyib sl 1, p 2 tog; rep from * around.

Work even 2 rnds in dk. Pull yarn through k sts slipping p sts to spare needle, then pull yarn through purl sts. Sew side seam of hand.

Baby's Lace Set, *Carol Rhoades*

CAROL RHOADES of Austin, Texas, combined two patterns in this cap and mitt set—the "Lace Star" pattern from a baby bonnet in a recent issue of *Knitters* magazine, and "Eyelet" from a Paton's leaflet ("Baby Styles from Beehive", #7117). "This cap is fairly easy to knit, and a nice way to show off a very special yarn," Carol says.

The set shown here is knitted in a fine, soft handspun yarn of blended Merino wool and kid mohair; Carol has also made it in wool and in a wool angora blend. "One friend liked it best with the purl side out!" she says.

For the intermediate knitter.

Size: Newborn.

Yarn: 2600 yd/lb (5226 m/kg), 18 wraps/in (28/4 cm). Carol's yarn is a lace-weight 2-ply handspun blend of Merino wool and kid mohair. The cap and mittens require only ¾ oz (21 g).

Gauge: With larger needle over lace pat 9 sts = 1 in (14 sts = 4 cm).

Needles: One set each of Size 1 (2½ mm) and 2 (2¾ mm) dpn or size to reach gauge given above.

Cap Instructions: With smaller needles cast on 7 sts. Join.

Rnd 1: (Yo, k 1, place marker) 7 times—14 sts.

Rnd 2 and all even-numbered rounds: Knit.

Rnd 3: (Yo, k 2) 7 times—21 sts.

Rnd 5: (Yo, k 3) 7 times—28 sts.

Rnd 7: (Yo, k 4) 7 times—35 sts.

Rnd 9: (Yo, k 5) 7 times—42 sts.

Rnd 11: (Yo, k 6) 7 times—49 sts.

Rnd 13: (Yo, k 5, k 2 tog) 7 times.

Rnd 15: (K 5, k 2 tog, yo) 7 times.

Rnd 17: (K 4, k 2 tog, yo, k 1, yo) 7 times—56 sts.

Rnd 19: (K 3, k 2 tog, yo, k 3, yo) 7 times—63 sts.

Rnd 21: (K 2, k 2 tog, yo, k 5, yo) 7 times—70 sts.

Rnd 23: (K 1, k 2 tog, yo, k 7, yo) 7 times—77 sts.

Rnd 25: (K 2 tog, yo, k 9, yo) 7 times—84 sts.

Rnd 26: Knit.

Next rnd: Change to larger needles, inc 6 sts evenly spaced around—90 sts. Divide sts on 3 needles.

Begin lace pat: Rnd 1: * K 2 tog, yo, k 1 in rnd below, yo, sl 1, k 1, psso, k 1; rep from * around.

Rnds 2, 3 and 4: Knit.

BABY'S LACE SET

Rep Rnds 1-4 for pat until pat length measures 3 in (8 cm) ending with Rnd 2. Work 6 rnds of k 2, p 2 ribbing, inc 2 st at beg of first rnd—92 sts.

Cast off *very* loosely. Using a Size 5 needles for the cast off will keep the edge loose.

Mitten Instructions: Cast on 36 sts. Join, being careful not to twist sts.

Rnd 1: * K 1, p 1; rep from * around.

Rnd 2: * P 1, k 1; rep from * around.

Rep these 2 rnds twice more.

Begin pattern: Rnd 1: * K 2 tog, yo, k 1 in row below, yo, skp, k 1; rep from * around.

Rnds 2, 3 and 4: Knit. Rep these 4 rnds for pat until total length is 1¾ in (4½ cm) ending with Rnd 2.

Next rnd: Inc in every 6th st around—42 sts. Continue in st st for 2 in (5 cm).

Finger tip shaping: Rnd 1: (K 1, k 2 tog) around—28 sts.

Rnds 2 and 4: Knit.

Rnd 3: K 2 tog around—14 sts.

Rnd 5: K 2 tog around—7 sts.

Thread end through rem sts and weave in end.

Bouncing Baby Set, *Jean Scorgie*

SIMPLE GARTER stitch sets off clever shaping in this set as humorous and squeezable as the best baby you know. Jean Scorgie of Denver, Colorado, derived the cap pattern from a Finnish one belonging to a friend. The knee socks, made to stay on, are like ones her brother had as an infant, and the thumbless mittens are simply obvious.

Jean is best known as a weaving teacher and designer, but calls herself a closet knitter. Her knitted designs always show thoughtful consideration for fit and construction, and a straightforward appreciation of her materials. Jean is a contributing editor to *Handwoven* magazine.

For the beginning knitter.

Size: Cap and mitts, up to 6 mo. Baby Legs instructions are given for 3 mo, with 6 and 9 mo in ( ).

Yarn: 1500 yd/lb (3000 m/kg), 20 wraps/in (31/4 cm). For the cap, Jean used 1 50-g (1½ oz) ball of Mayflower 4-ply cotton in a fingering weight. The baby legs and mitts are 2½ oz (75 g) of a similar weight yarn in a cotton-acrylic blend for better stretchiness, Pengouin Corrida 3.

Gauge: 7 sts = 1 in (11 sts = 4 cm).

Needles: Single-pointed needles size 2 (2.75–3 mm, 11) or size 3 (3.25 mm, 10) or size to reach gauge given above; crochet hook, size D or 3 (3 mm, 10).

Cap Instructions: Cast on 36 sts, leaving a 15 in (38 cm) tail for sewing later.

BOUNCING BABY SET

Row 1: K 2, inc 1 st by knitting in both front and back loop of next st, knit across to last 4 sts, k 2 tog, k 2.

Row 2: Knit.

Rows 3-32: Rep Row 1 and 2 for a total of 16 ridges. Place marker at beg of Row 32.

Row 33: K 2, k 2 tog, k across to last 3 sts, inc 1 st by knitting in both front and back loop of next st, k 2.

Row 34: Knit.

Rows 35-64: Rep Rows 33 and 34 (16 ridges from last marker). Place second marker at beg of Row 64.

Rows 65-80: Rep Rows 1 and 2 (8 ridges from last marker). Place third marker at beg of Row 80.

Rows 81-96: Rep Rows 33 and 34 (8 ridges from last marker). Place fourth marker at beg of Row 96.

Rows 97-128: Rep Rows 1 and 2 (16 ridges from last marker). Place fifth marker at beg of Row 128.

Rows 129–160: Rep Rows 33 and 34 (16 ridges from last marker). Bind off, leaving tail of 15 in (38 cm) for seaming.

Finishing: Identify edges as follows: Cast-on edge is A, bind off edge is B, cast on to first marker is C, between first and second markers is D, between second and third markers is E, between third and fourth markers is F, between fourth and fifth markers is G, between fifth marker and bind-off is H.

Using tail at end of cast-on, seam cast-on edge (A) to bind-off edge (B). Using tail at end of bind-off, seam edges H to G. With additional yarn seam edges C to D and E to F.

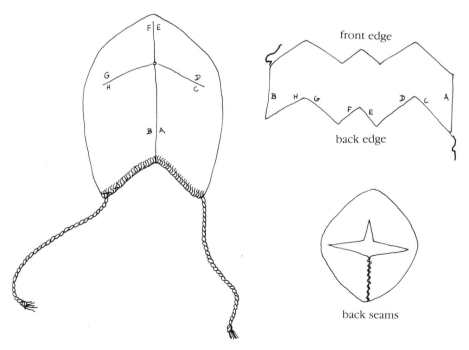

front edge

back edge

back seams

Ties (make 2): Cut 4 strands 30 in (76 cm) long. Fold strands in half and pull loop through point at side of cap. Draw ends through the loop forming a lark's head knot. Divide strands into 2 groups of 4. Twist each group tightly clockwise and twist them around each other in counter clockwise direction. Tie an overhand knot to join all 8 ends and trim ends evenly.

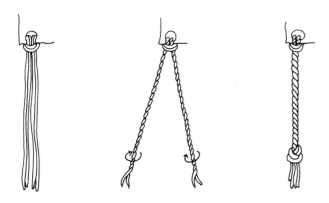

Baby Legs Instructions: Cast on 42 (48, 54) sts. K 2, p 2 for ¾ in (¾ in, 1 in) (2 cm, 2 cm, 2½ cm).

Shape knee as follows: k 28 (32, 36), turn the work, k 14 (16, 18). Turn, k 15 (17, 19), adding one st to the end of the row. Continue adding one st to the end of each row until there are 8 (10, 10) sts left at each side. Continue in this manner, adding 2 sts to the end of each row until all the sts are being knit.

Work straight for 16 (20, 24) rows until there are 8 (10, 12) ridges of garter st counted at the edge of the sock. Shape the leg by k 2 tog at each side every 4 rows 4 (5, 6) times. There will be 34 (38, 42) sts. Work straight until there are 8 (9, 10) ridges.

Work a tab for the top of the foot by k 23 (26, 28), turn, k 12 (14, 16). Work straight on these 12 (14, 16) sts for 6 (8, 10) ridges, then k 2 tog at each side of *each* row until all the sts are gone. Cut off yarn.

Reattach yarn at the right hand corner of the tab. There will be sts held on the needle at each side of the tab. Pick up sts around the tab, picking up 1½ sts per ridge at the sides and 2 sts per ridge across the point. K the sts held on the left needle, turn, k across entire row. Work even for 5 (5, 6) ridges.

Shape bottom of foot by k 2 tog at each side plus twice in the middle. Repeat this dec row every other row 4 times altogether. Bind off all sts; sew seam. Repeat for other sock.

Mitt Instructions: Cast on 36 sts. Work 10 rows of k 2, p 2 ribbing. Work eyelet row as follows: k 3, *yo, k 2 tog, k 2. Repeat from *, ending **k 1**. Work even in garter st for 13 ridges. Taper the top by k 2 tog at each side and twice in the middle. row, repeat dec row. Bind off. Sew seam.

Lacing Cord: Using crochet hook, ch 2, sc into first st 7 times, sl 1 to join in a circle. Chain 12 in (30 cm). In the 2nd st from the end, sc 7 times, sl to join, end off. Thread lace through eyelet. Repeat for other mitten.

Twisted Cord Ties

Twisted cord makes the easiest and quickest cap ties and mitten strings. Fasten two strands of yarn, each about 20% longer than you want the finished cord to be, in place on the knitted piece. An easy way to do this is to loop a piece of yarn twice as long as you want through the knit fabric with a lark's head knot.

With one tail in each hand, twist both in the *same* direction that the yarn is spun. This will be counter-clockwise in the case of most commercial yarns. Twist and twist until the yarn tries to kink up on itself. The amount of twist determines how firm the cord will be. Tie the two ends together with a slip knot, and release. The strands will ply themselves together. Smooth and even the twist out, and decorate the end with a tiny pompon, if you like.

If your yarn is very fine and you want a thicker cord, use two or three strands in place of each one.

Spiral Rib Mittens, *Mildred Oakey*

MILDRED OAKEY of Madison, Wisconsin, has been knitting these mittens for more than forty years. "I started making them for my two daughters and all their cousins. I am still making them for the next generation," she says.

Mildred's pattern is easily adaptable to many sizes by simply changing the needle size, yarn size, and/or number of stitches. (You can even leave off the thumb and wear them as tube socks!) There's no right or left hand, so they won't wear out unevenly. "In bitter cold weather," she says, "we slip one mitten inside another for extra warmth."

For the intermediate knitter.

Size: 4-year-old child. Changes for adult size follow in parentheses.

Yarn: 1000 yd/lb (2010 m/kg), 12 wraps/in (19/4 cm). Mildred used 1 4-oz (113 g) skein of knitting worsted for each pair of mittens.

Gauge: Over pat st 6 sts = 1 in (9 sts = 4 cm); 7 rows = 1 in (11 rows = 4 cm).

Needles: One set of dpn, size 3 (3.25 mm, 10) or size to reach given above.

Instructions: Cuff: Cast on 32 (40) sts; divide on 3 needles. Join, work around in k 1, p 1 rib for child, (k 2, p 2 rib for adult) for 14 (18) rnds. Mark last st as end of rnd.

Hand pattern: Rnds 1–3: (P 2, k 2) around.

Rnds 4–6: K 1, (p 2, k 2) around to last 3 sts, end with p 2, k 1.

Rnds 7–9: (K 2, p 2) around.

Rnds 10–12: P 1, (k 2, p 2) around to last 3 sts, end k 2, p 1.

Adult only: Rep Rnds 1–12.

Thumb opening: Both sizes: Continue with pat as established and at the same time on next rnd, sl first 6 (8) sts to holder for thumb. Cast on 6 (8) sts. Continue in pattern as established until 24 (36) rnds of pat st are completed from beg of thumb opening ending with Rnd 12 of pat st.

Finger tip shaping: Rnd 1: Continue in pat, working (p 2, k 2) around.

Rnd 2: (P 2 tog, k 2) around—24 (30) sts.

Rnd 3: (P 1, k 2) around.

Rnds 4–6: K 1, (p 1, k 2) around to last 2 sts, end p 1, k 1.

Rnd 7: (K 2, p 1) around.

Rnd 8: (K 2 tog, p 1) around—16 (20) sts.

Rnd 9: (K 1, p 1) around.

Rnd 10: (P 1, k 1) around.

Rnd 11: K 2 tog around—8 (10) sts.

Break off, leaving an end. Draw end through all 8 (10) sts twice. Draw together tightly. Fasten off.

Thumb: Rnd 1: Sl 6 (8) thumb sts from the holder to needle; pick up 8 (12) sts along cast-on edge of thumb opening—14 (20) sts. Divide these sts on 3 needles and work around in st st for 12 (18) rnds.

Decrease for thumb, child size only: **Rnd 1:** (K 2, k 2 tog) around to last 2 sts, k 2—11 sts. **Rnds 2 and 3:** Knit. **Rnd 4:** (K 2 tog, k 1) around to last 2 sts, k 2—8 sts. **Rnd 5:** Knit. **Rnd 6:** K 2 tog around—4 sts. Break off, leaving an end. Draw end through all 4 sts twice. Draw together tightly. Fasten off. Make other mitten identically. Attach with double chain mitten cord.

Dec for thumb, adult size only: **Rnd 1:** (K 2, k 2 tog) around—15 sts. **Rnds 2 and 3:** Knit. **Rnd 4:** (K 1, k 2 tog) around— 10 sts. **Rnd 5:** Knit. **Rnd 6:** K 2 tog around—5 sts. Break off, leaving an end. Draw end through all 5 sts twice. Draw together tightly; fasten off. Make other mitten identically.

Double Chain Mitten String

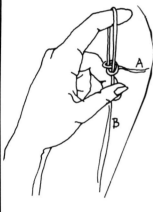

This is one of those tricks that's harder to talk about than to do. Once you've gotten the hang of it, you'll be able to make mitten strings with your eyes closed!

Measure a length of yarn about nine times as long as the finished length you want. Make a slip knot at the halfway point. Insert your left index finger into the loop of the knot (figure 1). Important: **End B is the one that tightens the loop when pulled.**

Holding the knot between left thumb and middle finger, insert right index finger into the front of the loop, and draw through a new loop with End A (figure 2). Hold knot lightly with right thumb and middle finger while you pull on End B to tighten up the first loop. Insert left index finger into front of loop, and draw through a new loop with End B (figure 3). Hold the knot lightly with left thumb and middle finger while you pull on End A to tighten up the last loop. Continue in this way to make the string.

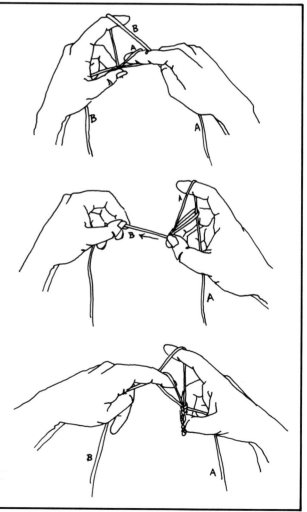

Family Mittens, *Lucy Rogers*

LUCY ROGERS of Bethel, Maine, developed these patterns especially for speedy knitting on large needles. The body of the mittens uses a double strand of yarn and #10 needles, so the mittens are thick and durable for Maine winters and easy enough for beginning knitters.

The pattern has been ideal for Lucy's business, Hilltop Handspuns, which sells handspun yarns and handmade knitwear. She has had the pattern printed up and sells it along with her lovely soft, tweedy yarn. The yarn is a singles about the same size as a commercial knitting worsted, spun from natural colors of imported Romney carded together. Each pair requires a hundred yards of yarn.

For the beginning knitter.

Size: 2- to 4-year-old child, and adult small (medium, large).

Yarn: 800 yd/lb (1600 m/kg), 12 wraps/in (19/4 cm). Lucy used a soft handspun single-ply wool similar to Lopi, but less regular in diameter. She carded together natural grays and white for a tweedy effect. The child's mittens require 2 oz (56 g), and the adult sizes require about 4 oz (113 g).

Gauge: With larger needles over stockinette st 7 sts = 2 in (11 st = 8 cm).

Needles: One set of dpn, size 10 (6–6.5 mm, 3) or size to reach gauge given above; one set of dpn, size 6 (4–4.5 mm, 7); small stitch holder.

Child's Mitten Instructions: With smaller needles cast on 24 sts. Work k 1, p 1 rib for 18 rnds. Change to st st and larger needles and add another strand of yarn from the other end of the ball (wind ball so that yarn is available from both ends). Knit 7 rnds plain.

Thumb gusset: At beg of next rnd, inc 1 st in first st, k 3, inc 1 st in next st, k to end of rnd—26 sts. Knit 2 more rnds. Sl first 7 sts of rnd to holder for thumb. Join rem sts for hand—19 sts. Knit 12 rnds plain, then begin finger tip shaping.

Finger tip shaping: (K 2 tog, k 2) 4 times, k 3—15 sts. Knit 1 rnd plain.

Next rnd: (K 1, k 2 tog) around—10 sts.

Following rnd: K 2 tog around—5 sts. K 2 tog once (this is a partial rnd)—4 sts. Fasten off.

Thumb: Divide 7 thumb sts on 3 needles; pick up 2 sts on inside of thumb—9 sts. Work 1 rnd. **Next rnd:** Dec 1 st by knitting 2 tog—8 sts. Knit 8 rnds.

Dec for thumb: K 2 tog around—4 sts. Fasten off. Make second mitten the same.

Adult Mitten Instructions: With smaller needles cast on 32 (34, 36) sts. Divide on 3 needles. Work in k 1, p 1 rib for 4 in (10 cm).

Thumb gusset: Rnd 1: Change to st st and knit next rnd, dec 6 sts evenly spaced around—26 (28, 30) sts. Change to larger needles and add a second strand of yarn (wind ball so yarn is available from both ends).

Rnd 2: Inc 1 st in first st, k 1, inc 1 st in next st, k to end of rnd—28 (30, 32) sts.

Rnds 3 and 4: Knit.

Rnd 5: Inc 1 st in first st, k 3, inc 1 st in next st, k to end of rnd—30 (32, 34) sts.

Rnds 6 and 7: Knit.

Rnd 8: Inc 1 st in first st, k 5, inc 1 st in next st, k to end of rnd—32 (34, 36) sts.

Rnds 9 and 10: Knit.

Rnd 11: Inc 1 st in first st, k 7, inc 1 st in next st, k to end of rnd—34 (36, 38) sts.

Rnds 12 and 13: Knit.

Thumb opening: Sl first 11 sts of rnd to holder for thumb. Cast on 1 st and join for hand—24 (26, 28) sts. Knit to within 1 in (2½ cm) of desired length.

Finger tip shaping: Rnd 1: (K 2, k 2 tog) around (size medium only, end k 2)—18 (20, 21) sts.

Rnd 2: Knit.

Rnd 3: (K 1, k 2 tog) around (Size medium only, end k 2)—12 (14, 14) sts.

Rnd 4: K 2 tog around—6 (7, 7) sts.

Rnd 5: K 2 tog two (three, three) times (this is a partial rnd)—4 sts. Fasten off.

Thumb: Divide 11 thumb sts from holder on 3 needles. Pick up 2 sts on inside of thumb—13 sts. Work even 1 rnd. On next rnd dec 1 st on inside of thumb—12 sts. Knit to desired length.

Dec for thumb: Next rnd: K 2 tog around—6 sts.

Following rnd: K 2 tog twice (this is a partial rnd) 4—sts.

Fasten off. Make second mitten the same.

Honeycomb Mittens, *Jean Newsted*

L AST SUMMER I spent many happy afternoons dyeing small amounts of fleece with natural dyestuffs gathered from the Alberta countryside and my own garden," writes Jean Newsted of Calgary, Alberta. "This delightful pastime left me with a lot of lovely bits of yarn. I designed these honeycomb mittens to use and show off these pretty colors."

Jean's mittens are constructed in a straight tube without increases for the thumb, so you might want to make them in a larger size than usual. Jean notes that the ladies' size small is just right for her thirteen year old daughter who has long, slender hands.

For another variation on the Honeycomb stitch, see Lizbeth Upitis' Cathedral Mittens on page 114.

For the intermediate knitter.

Size: Women's small. Changes for women's medium and large follow in parentheses.

Yarn: 700 yd/lb (1400 m/kg), 14 wraps/in (22/4 cm). Jean spun a two-ply yarn from very lustrous long wool that looks almost like mohair; it is heavy for its diameter. A commercial sport-weight yarn would be a suitable substitute. She used 3 oz (85 g) of natural white (MC) and about 10 yd (9 m) of each of the six honeycomb pattern colors.

Gauge: Over honeycomb pattern 6 sts = 1 in (9 sts = 4 cm).

Needles: One set of dpn, size 4 (3.5 mm, 9) or size to reach gauge given above.

Instructions: Honeycomb pattern: Rnd 1: With MC knit.

Rnd 2: With MC purl.

Rnds 3-8: With CC * K 4, sl 2; rep from * around.

Rnd 9: With MC knit.

Rnd 10: With MC purl.

Rnds 11-16: With different CC k 1, * sl 2, k 4; rep from * around to last 5 sts end sl 2, k 3.

Rep Rnds 1-16 for honeycomb pattern.

Right mitten: With MC cast on 40 (46, 52) sts. Divide on 3 needles. Work in twisted rib as follows: **Rnd 1:** * K 1 in back lp, p 1; rep from * around.

Rnd 2: * K 1, purl 1; rep from * around.

Repeat these 2 rnds for total of 20 rnds, inc 8 sts evenly spaced on last rnd of rib—48 (54, 60) sts.

Next rnd: Begin honeycomb pat. When 32 rnds of pat are completed, establish place for thumb opening by working next 2 rnds as follows: **Rnd 1:** With MC, knit.

Rnd 2: With MC, p 1, with piece of scrap yarn p 6 (7, 8) sts. Sl these 6 (7, 8) sts back to left needle and purl them again with MC; complete rnd.

After you have completed the body of the mitten you will remove the scrap yarn to create an opening for the thumb. Have faith—this really works. Continue in honeycomb pat until you have completed 48 (48, 56) rnds past thumb opening.

Finger tip shaping: Change to st st and complete finger tip shaping with MC only as follows:

Next rnd: * K 4, k 2 tog; rep from * around—40 (45, 50) sts.

Next 4 rnds: Knit.

Next rnd: * K 3, k 2 tog; rep from * around—32 (36, 40) sts.

Next 3 rnds: Knit.

Next rnd: * K 2, k 2 tog; rep from * around—24 (27, 30) sts.

Next 2 rnds: Knit.

Next rnd: K 1, k 2 tog; rep from * around—16 (18, 20).

Next rnd: Knit.

Next rnd: K 2 tog around—8 (9, 10) sts.

Break off yarn, leaving 6 in (15 cm) end. Thread yarn end through tapestry needle and run needle through remaining sts, drawing them up tightly. Fasten off.

Thumb: Carefully remove piece of scrap yarn. This will expose 5 (6, 7) loops on top of thumb opening and another 6 (7, 8) loops on bottom of opening. Sl these loops to 3 dpn, picking up 2 sts at each end of opening—15 (17, 19) sts. Work 15 (17, 19) rnds.

Thumb shaping: Rnd 1: * (K 1, k 2 tog) around, end k 0 (2, 1)—10 (12, 13) sts.

Rnd 2: Knit.

Rnd 3: K 2 tog around end k 0 (0, 1)—5 (6, 7) sts.

Break yarn and draw through rem sts. Fasten off. Turn mitten inside out and carefully darn in all ends.

Left Mitten: Work ribbing and first 32 rnds of honeycomb pat as for right mitten. To create thumb opening, work as follows: **Rnd 1:** Knit with MC.

Rnd 2: Purl next rnd to last 7 (8, 9) sts on last needle. Purl next 6 (7, 8) sts with piece of scrap yarn. Place these 6 (7, 8) sts back to left needle and purl them with MC; purl 1.

Complete as for right mitten.

Natural Dyes For Knitting Yarns

Nothing personalizes a knitting project quite so much as hand dyed yarn. The pattern colors in Jean's Honeycomb Mittens came from Russian tarragon (green), Saskatoon berries (lavender and purple), wood shavings (rose), red snapdragons (goldish beige), and small brown mushrooms (yellow). Other possibilities: marigold blossoms (gold), yellow onion skins (brass), red cosmos blossoms (rusty red), coffee grounds (taupe), tea leaves (tan). Almost any plant will yield color, though many tend toward uninteresting beiges and tans. Consult the bibliography on page 161 for books on natural dyes, and don't be afraid to experiment.

Most natural dyestuffs will take only on natural fibers, especially wool. Most require that the yarn be soaked in a "mordant" so the fiber will take up the color. Here's an easy one-pot recipe for dyeing an ounce of yarn.

Old gold marigold dyepot

Simmer a quart of marigold blossoms and one and a half quarts of water together in a stainless steel or enamel pan for 20 minutes. Keep temperature very low—below 180°.

Meanwhile, soak an ounce of white or natural wool yarn in hot, soapy tap water.

Scoop flowers out of pan, and add 1½ teaspoons of alum (available in the canning or spice department at your grocery store) to the pan as a mordant.

Rinse yarn gently in hot tap water, and add to pan. Put on very low heat, just under a simmer, stirring gently occasionally, for 30 minutes or longer.

Let yarn cool in the dyebath. When it's cooled to lukewarm, remove yarn, rinse gently until water runs clear, blot excess moisture in a towel, and hang in a shady spot to dry.

Lover's Mittens & Glittens, *Jeanne McCanless*

W HEN YOU ARE young and walk along holding hands with someone very special," writes Jeanne McCanless, "the mittens needed to keep hands warm in winter make holding hands a rather impersonal thing." So Jeanne invented this special solution for her teenagers.

Four ounces of knitting worsted make two regular mittens and a special one to share. Another four-ounce skein is more than enough for another of Jeanne's creations, "Glittens"—mittens with a finger. "When my daughter was in high school the building was so cold that she wore her mittens all day to keep her hands warm," Jeanne says. "Since it was hard to hold a pencil with mittens on, she asked me to put a finger in her mittens." Over the years, Jeanne has shared this pattern with many other knitters who have found them as versatile as gloves, but as warm as mittens, for hunting, doing outdoor chores, or tying ice skates.

Jeanne divides her time between her small yarn shop and a herd of Angora goats in Oskaloosa, Iowa; she looks forward to the day when she'll be knitting her mittens with her own handspun yarn.

For the intermediate knitter.

Size: Adult medium.

Yarn: 1000 yd/lb (2010 m/kg), 12 wraps/in (19/4 cm). Jeanne used 1 4-oz (113 g) skein of 4-ply knitting worsted to make 1 pair of standard mittens plus one Lover's Mitten. A pair of Glittens also requires 1 skein.

Gauge: With larger needles over stockinette st, 11 sts = 2 in (8½ sts = 4 cm).

Needles: Two sets of dpn, one each in size 3 (3.25 mm, 10) and size 5 (3.75–4 mm, 8) or size to reach gauge given above.

Instructions: The following instructions for the Lovers' Mitten are derived from Jeanne's favorite mitten pattern. You can easily adapt any mitten pattern, such as Jackie Fee's Mushroom Mittens on page 68, to this style, and then make two regular mittens to complete the set.

Knit the cuff of standard 4-needle mitten. Change to larger needles and increase (if called for); work even for 1 in (2½ cm). Put this cuff on holders and make another cuff exactly like the first.

Joining cuffs: Sl ⅓ of sts from first cuff to a double-pointed needle, sl ⅓ of sts from second cuff to another double-pointed needle. Jeanne's cuffs each had 42 sts, so she put 14 sts from each cuff on dpn. Hold the cuffs with right sides together and knit these sts tog in a knitted seam as follows: With a third needle, k 2 tog twice, each time using 1 st from the front needle with 1 st from the back needle. Sl first st over second st. Continue in this way to k 2 tog once, then bind off one st until all 28 sts are used. To bind off last st, k 1 st from holder, pass last st over this st. Sl rem 55 sts from holders to dpn, dividing sts evenly—56 sts. Jeanne finds that it's easier to work with 5 needles rather than the traditional 4 at this point, if you have an extra needle in the same size.

Hand: Change to st st and work even for about 1½ in (4 cm), then inc 9 sts evenly spaced around—65 sts. Continue to work even until length is 1 in (2½ cm) less than desired finished length.

Duplicate Stitch or Swiss Darning

Add an isolated pattern motif or a third color to two color knitting with duplicate stitch—a technique for covering existing stitches with a pattern yarn. Use a yarn of the same diameter as the base fabric, but in a contrasting color or fuzzy texture.

Thread a tapestry needle with the pattern yarn and, from the inside, pull the yarn through the center of the stitch below the one to be covered. Pass the needle under both sides of the stitch above the one to be covered, and back down through the center of the one below. Move to the next stitch, and repeat.

Essentially, you are simply following the path of each stitch that is to be covered. It's as simple as that.

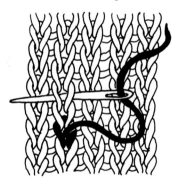

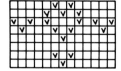

Decrease for finger tip: Rnd 1: (K 2 tog, k 3) around—52 sts.

    Rnds 2, 4 and 6: Work even.

    Rnd 3: (K 2 tog, k 2) around)—39 sts.

    Rnd 5: (K 2 tog, k 1) around—26 sts.

    Rnd 7: K 2 tog around—13 sts.

    Rnd 8: K 2 tog around, end k 1—7 sts.

Draw yarn through last sts and pull up tightly. Fasten off securely. Since patterns vary, there may be an odd st in the dec rows. Because you are really making a large pouch it doesn't make all that much difference.

Use contrasting color yarn to work heart motifs with duplicate st.

GLITTENS

Glitten Instructions: Using smaller needles cast on 40 sts. Divide on three needles and join, being careful not to twist sts. Work in k 2, p 2 ribbing for 3 in (8 cm). Change to larger needles and st st, inc 2 sts on first rnd—42 sts. Work even for 3 rnds.

Shape thumb gusset: Rnd 1: K 5, place marker, inc in each of next 2 sts, place marker, k to end of rnd—44 sts.

Rnd 2 and all even-numbered rnds: Knit.

Rnd 3: K to first marker, inc in next st, k to 1 st before second marker, inc in next st, k to end of rnd. Rep Rnds 2 and 3 until there are 12 sts bet markers, ending with Rnd 2—52 sts. Work even for 4 rnds more.

Rnd 4: K to first marker, sl next 12 sts to holder to be worked later for thumb, cast on 2 sts to replace these sts, k to end of rnd—42 sts.

Work even for 12 rnds more (or length needed to first finger).

Next rnd: Work 12 sts and sl these 12 sts to holder for finger. Complete rnd—30 sts.

Cast on 4 sts to replace finger sts and continue working even on these 34 sts until piece measures 1 in (2½ cm) less than desired finished length.

Finger tip shaping: Rnd 1: K 4, * k 2 tog, k 4; rep from * to end of rnd—29 sts.

Rnd 2 and all even-numbered rnds through Rnd 8: Knit.

Rnd 3: K 4, * k 2 tog, k 3; rep from * to end of rnd—24 sts.

Rnd 5: K 4, * k 2 tog, k 2; rep from * around—19 sts.

Rnd 7: K 4, * k 2 tog, k 1; rep from * around—14 sts.

Rnd 9: K 4, (k 2 tog, k 1) 3 times, end k 1—11 sts.

Rnd 10: K 2 tog around, end k 1—6 sts.

Break off yarn leaving end. Draw yarn through last sts and pull up tightly. Fasten off securely.

Thumb: Sl 12 sts from holder to larger needles, join yarn and pick up 3 sts over cast-on sts—15 sts. (If you want, pick up one extra st at each corner to help prevent holes at these corners and k 2 tog at each corner on the next rnd.) Continue in st st until thumb measures ½ in (1 cm) from desired finished length.

Thumb dec: Rnd 1: * K 2 tog, k 1; rep from * around—10 sts.

Rnd 2: Knit.

Rnd 3: (K 2 tog) around—5 sts.

Break off yarn, leaving end, and finish as before.

Finger: Sl 12 sts from holder to larger needles, join yarn and pick up 3 sts (or 5 as before)—15 sts. Complete as for thumb.

Fingerless Mitts, *Phyllis Rodgers*

PHYLLIS RODGERS of Hingham, Massachusetts, has a beautiful, scholarly daughter whose hands are always cold—especially when she studies. Hence these fingerless mitts, equally suitable for musicians in unheated garrets, computer operators in chilly offices, knitters in drafty corners—let your imagination dictate the design!

Phyllis referred to a crochet pattern in an old 1915 Bear Brand booklet, and adapted them to knitting with her own handspun yarn. "I wonder how they would be for the southern climes in a cotton lace pattern—for beauty, or for sweaty palms?" she speculates. Try these in various rib patterns, and finish the edges with single crochet or crocheted scallop edging, too.

For the beginning knitter.

Size: One size fits all.

Yarn: 1000 yd/lb (2010 m/kg), 12 wraps/in (19/4 cm). Phyllis used a 2-ply handspun Montadale cross similar in weight to a 4-ply knitting worsted. Her mitts require about 1½ oz (42 g), and a small amount of contrasting yarn for embroidered trim.

Gauge: Over garter st 5 sts = 1 in (8 sts = 4 cm); 10 rows = 1 in (16 rows = 4 cm).

Needles: One pair, size 6 (4–4.5 mm, 7) or size to reach gauge given above.

Instructions: Cast on 36 sts. **Row 1 (wrong side):** Knit 2, work loop st as follows: * Wind yarn around middle finger as it's held behind work to form loop, k 1 but do not remove st from left needle; sl st just formed to left needle, remove finger from loop and k 2 tog (st just formed and next st) through back lps; rep from * twice more, k to end of row.

Row 2: Knit.

Row 3: Rep Row 1.

Row 4: Knit.

Row 5: Work 3 loop sts, k to end of row.

Row 6: Knit.

Rep Rows 5 and 6 until there is a total of 16 ridges (32 rows).

Thumb opening: Row 33: Work 3 loop sts, k 6, bind off 6 for thumb opening, k to end of row—30 sts.

Row 34: K 21, cast on 6 sts, k to end of row—36 sts.

Rep Rows 5 and 6 16 times. There is a total of 33 ridges (66 rows). With wrong side facing, fold work so cast-on row is behind last row worked. Insert needle through first st on needle and through first cast-on st, k them together; repeat for next st on needle and next cast-on st. Pass previous st over last st worked. Continue across, knitting last row worked and cast-on row together and binding off at the same time.

Embroider flower motif using "lazy daisy" and french knot stitches near loop sts of Rows 1 through 4.

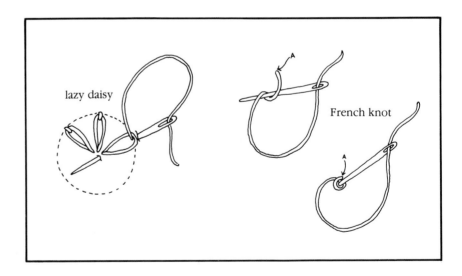

Sideways Mystery Mittens,

Elizabeth Zimmermann

WITH THE HEART of a knitter and the mind of a sculptor, or perhaps an engineer, Elizabeth Zimmermann has come up with a completely original approach to the homely old mitten. Knitted flat in garter stitch (anything to avoid a purl!), this unlikely piece of knitting looks as though it could become almost anything *but* a mitten, until a few strategic seams give it its final shape.

Elizabeth's approach to knitting instructions, well known to fans of *Knitting Without Tears* and her other writings, is to give a conceptual account of how to achieve a piece, and then follow that up with more specific instructions for "Blind Followers"—those of us who prefer a little more hand holding.

Elizabeth's books (see Bibliography), articles, videotapes, semiannual newsletters, workshops, and summer knitting camps all speak of the energy, ingenuity, inspiration, and humor that have shaped a whole generation of handknitters.

For the intermediate knitter.

Size: Medium.

Yarn: 840 yd/lb (1688 m/kg), 12 wraps/in (19/4 cm). Elizabeth used 1 4-oz (113 g) skein of 2-ply Sheepswool, but suggests 4-ply Fisherman yarn or Icelandic Lopi as good alternatives.

Gauge: Over garter st 5 sts = 1 in (8 sts = 4 cm).

Needles: One pair, to reach gauge given above; sizes will generally range from 4 (3.5 mm, 9) to 7 (4.5–5 mm, 6).

(Editor's note: We have not used the customary ( )'s to shorten a pattern in order to have a more visual presentation of these instructions. We feel this will help in constructing this very complex and intriguing design. We have provided Elizabeth's usual succinct instructions, plus her "Blind Follower Instructions" for those knitters who are more comfortable with detailed directions.)

Instructions: Beg at "inseam" of thumb and first finger cast on 57 sts.

Row 1 (wrong side): K 10 for thumb, p 1, k 1, p 1, k 15 for forefinger, p 1 (center st), then reverse matters: k 15, p 1, k 1, p 1, k 10. Mark these 5 purled sts; to identify them later, we'll call the center st C, the 2 marked sts each side of it B and the outermost 2 marked sts A. These marked sts are always purled on the wrong side, which makes a k chain on the right side—an elegant line and a guide for shaping. On odd-numbered rows purl the marked sts and k all other sts.

Knitting Theorists: On even-numbered rows all sts are k and M1's are made; on Rows 2 through 10 these M1's are made to the inside of A and each side of B and C.

Blind Follower Instructions: Row 2: K 11, *make backward lp on right needle (M1 completed)*, k 1, M1, k 1, M1, k 15, M1, k 1, M1, k 15, M1, k 1, M1, k 1, M1, k 11—65 sts.

Row 3 and all odd numbered rows: P marked sts, k all other sts.

Row 4: K 11, M1, k 3, M1, k 1, M1, k 17, M1, k 1, M1, k 17, M1, k 1, M1, k 3, M1, k 11—73 sts.

Row 6: K 11, M1, k 3, M1, k 1, M1, k 19, M1, k 1, M1, k 19, M1, k 1, M1, k 5, M1, k 11—81 sts.

Row 8: K 11, M1, k 7, M1, k 1, M1, k 21, M1, k 1, M1, k 21, M1, k 1, M1, k 7, M1, k 11—89 sts.

Row 10: K 11, M1, k 9, M1, k 1, M1, k 21, M1, k 1, M1, k 21, M1, k 1, M1, k 9, M1, k 11—97 sts.

Knitting Theorists: When you have 5½ ridges (11 rows) end the incs each side of st C, but continue to purl C on odd-numbered rows.

Blind Follower Instructions: Row 12: K 11, M1, k 11, M1, k 1, M1, k 51, M1, k 1, M1, k 11, M1, k 11—103 sts.

Row 14: K 11, M1, k 13, M1, k 1, M1, k 53, M1, k 1, M1, k 13, M1, k 11—109 sts.

Row 16: K 11, M1, k 15, M1, k 1, M1, k 55, M1, k 1, M1, k 15, M1, k 11—115 sts.

Knitting Theorists: When you have 8 ridges (16 rows) thumb is completed. Remove 10 sts at each end of needle to holders for thumb, remove markers from A, end incs to the inside of A, continue incs each side of B and begin dec 1 st at end of each row.

Blind Follower Instructions: Row 17: K 10 and sl to holder for one side of thumb, k 18, p 1, k 28, p 1, k 28, p 1, k 16, k 2 tog. Sl rem 10 sts to holder for other side of thumb—94 sts.

Row 18: K 17, M1, k 1, M1, k 57, M1, k 1, M1, k 16, k 2 tog—97 sts.

Row 19: K 18, p 1, k 29, p 1, k 29, p 1, k 16, k 2 tog—96 sts.

Row 20: K 17, M1, k 1, M1, k 59, M1, k 1, M1, k 16, k 2 tog—99 sts.

Row 21: K 18, p 1, k 30, p 1, k 30, p 1, k 16, k 2 tog—98 sts.

Knitting Theorists: When you have 10½ ridges (21 rows), begin to dec 1 st each side of C, continue to dec 1 st at end of every row and continue to inc each side of B.

Blind Follower Instructions: Row 22: K 17, M1, k 1, M1, k 29, *sl 2 tog as to k, k 1, p2sso (double dec completed)*, k 29, M1, k 1, M1, k 16, k 2 tog—99 sts.

Row 23: K 18, p 1, k 30, p 1, k 30, p 1, k 16, k 2 tog—98 sts.

Row 24: K 17, M1, k 1, M1, k 29, double dec, k 29, M1, k 1, M1, k 16, k 2 tog—99 sts.

Row 25: K 18, p 1, k 30, p 1, k 30, p 1, k 16, k 2 tog—98 sts.

Row 26: K 17, M1, k 1, M1, k 29, double dec, k 29, M1, k 1, M1, k 16, k 2 tog—99 sts.

Row 27: K 18, p 1, k 30, p 1, k 30, p 1, k 16, k 2 tog—98 sts.

Row 28: K 17, M1, k 1, M1, k 29, double dec, k 29, M1, k 1, M1, k 16, k 2 tog—99 sts.

Row 29: K 18, p 1, k 30, p 1, k 30, p 1, k 16, k 2 tog—98 sts.

Row 30: K 17, M1, k 1, M1, k 29, double dec, k 29, M1, k 1, M1, k 16, k 2 tog—99 sts.

Knitting Theorists: When you have 15 ridges (30 rows) end dec at end of row and end incs each side of B. Work to center of next right-side row and make double dec.

Blind Follower|Instructions: Row 31: K 18, p 1, k 30, p 1, k 30, p 1, k 18.

Row 32: K 48, double dec; do not finish row.

All knitters: Fold work so finger tip of mitten is at right. Work garter st weaving up to and including B; join yarn and complete row. Rem sts are for wrist and cuff.

Wrist and cuff: Knit 6 ridges (12 rows). Inc for cuff by working (k 2, M1) across. Work even as long as wanted for cuff. Cast off in purl on the right side leaving a generous tail. Sew side seam. Weave thumb. L and R hands are the same. Give them in threes.

Lambsheep Mittens, *Jamie Ledford*

JAMIE LEDFORD of Franklin, Tennessee, adapted these mittens from an old pattern that was a favorite of her mother's. She created the first pair for her daughter (who gave them their name), but has since worked them up in a wide range of sizes simply by changing yarn and needle size.

"I learned to knit from my mother when I was young," Jamie says, "but didn't become a compulsive knitter until nine years ago. Now I have at least two projects going all the time." Jamie has recently taken up spinning and dyeing, and used some of her handspun scraps for the "topknot" on these charming mittens.

For the beginning knitter.

Size: Child's. Larger sizes can be made using heavier yarn and larger needles and following same pattern.

Yarn: 1000 yd/lb (2010 m/kg), 12-14 wraps/in (19-22/4 cm). Jamie used 1 skein of Reynolds Lopi Light, a softly spun single-ply yarn. Features are embroidered with cotton embroidery floss, and "curls" are scraps of handspun natural black wool.

Gauge: Over stockinette st, 5 sts = 1 in (8 sts = 4 cm).

Needles: One set of dpn, size 5 (3.75–4 mm, 8) or size to reach gauge given above.

Instructions: Cast on 38 sts and divide on 3 needles. Join and work k 1, p 1 rib for 28 rnds, inc 2 sts in last rnd—40 sts.

Change to st st and knit evenly until 13 rnds of st st have been completed.

Opening for "ears": Rnd 14: K 13, bind off 7 sts for little finger (1 st remains on right needle), k 12 more (for a total of 13 sts following bind off), bind off last 7 sts of rnd for thumb. (Note: You will need to use first st of Rnd 15 to complete bind-off of last st)—26 sts.

Rnd 15: Knit to first group of 7 bound-off sts, cast on 7 sts, knit to second group of 7 bound-off sts, cast on 7 sts—40 sts.

Knit until you have 18 rnds completed from separation for little finger and thumb.

Fingertip decs: Rnd 1: (K 8, k 2 tog) 4 times—36 sts.

>**Rnd 2:** Knit.

>**Rnd 3:** (K 4, k 2 tog) 6 times—30 sts.

>**Rnds 4 and 5:** Knit.

>**Rnd 6:** (K 3, k 2 tog) 6 times—24 sts.

>**Rnds 7 and 8:** Knit.

>**Rnd 9:** (K 4, k 2 tog) 4 times—20 sts.

>**Rnd 10 and 11:** Knit.

Break off yarn, draw through rem sts and close.

Thumb and little finger: Pick up 7 sts along bind-off edge; pick up 8 sts along cast-on edge—15 sts. Knit even for 12 rnds or until thumb (or finger) is long enough, K 2 tog around, end k 1—8 sts. Cut yarn, draw through sts and tie off.

Embroider face: With yarn work bullion knots for the "curls." With embroidery floss work satin stitch for eyes and stem stitch for nose and mouth.

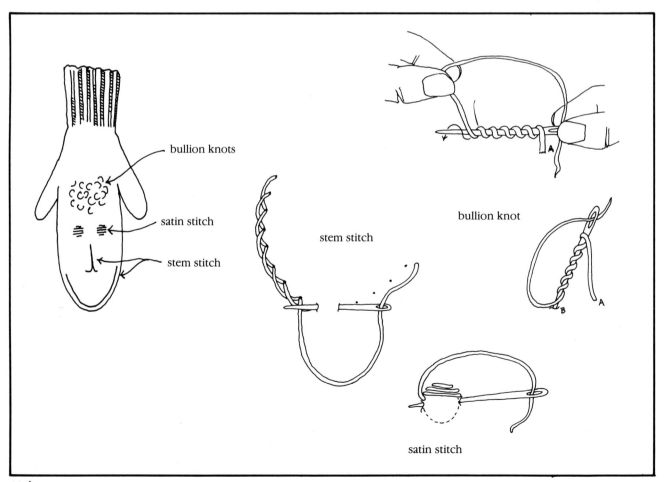

bullion knots

satin stitch

stem stitch

stem stitch

bullion knot

satin stitch

Kennebunk Wooly Bear Mittens

Robin Hansen

W HEN ROBIN HANSEN's book, *Fox & Geese & Fences*, was published in 1983, it created a new level of appreciation for traditional home knitting. Sturdy, warm, lively mittens for work and play, taken for granted for generations, revealed their stories as she gently probed their history and techniques. Patterns like Salt & Pepper, Sawtooth, and Spruce have become old friends to knitters everywhere.

If you've tried Robin's pattern for Fleece Stuffed Mittens, you'll find a special challenge in her Kennebunk Wooly Bear Mittens; the unusual shagging technique creates a fabric of unequalled resilience and warmth. Here's Robin's story:

Shagging is what makes this mitten special. There were many kinds of shagged mittens during the 1700s and 1800s, some with knitted-in shag, some with sewn-on shag, some shagged on the inside, others on the outside, some with raw fleece, others with the leftovers of warp threads left from weaving. Most were very bulky and had to be removed for any but the coarsest manipulation; they could be used for driving horses, but not for putting on the bridle.

Shagged mittens were once made throughout New England and the maritime provinces of Canada. In Labrador and Newfoundland today, women commonly catch little bits of raw fleecee into their knitting in both mittens, caps, and occasionally vests, to add to their thickness and warmth. I know of only a single traditional knitter in New Hampshire, and another in upper New York state, who knit loops of raw fleece into their mittens, but no one who actually sews yarn on afterward as the original knitter of these mittens did.

The original pair of mittens came through my back door one morning in the hands of Maine State folklorist Amanda McQuiddy, who was taking them to be exhibited in the Governor's Gallery at the Maine State House in Augusta. She thought I might be interested.

They came from the Brick Store Museum in Kennebunk and had no documentation at all; there's no record of who knit them, for whom, when, or where. It's likely, however, that they were knitted in New England, probably in Maine, and because of the fineness of the knit, McQuiddy thinks, probably in the 1800s. Although diary accounts tell of shagged mittens knitted in the 1700s in New England, few have survived, and most are not datable.

I was delighted; I had never seen such mittens, thick but finely knit, flexible and warm. We turned one inside out immediately to find out how it was made, saw that the shag followed the ribs exactly from cuff edge to

Original mittens courtesy of Brick Store Museum, Kennebunk, Maine.

tip, and determined that it was not knitted in, as no yarn was carried between the ribs. The clincher was that a tightly curled little end of yarn began each column of shagging at the cuff. I couldn't wait to make one!

The original mittens were knit at a tension of 13 sts to an inch. I found a pair of Size 0000 needles and tried to knit a little square to see if I would get the same tension. The sport weight yarn I was using was too softly spun for such fine knitting, and the sharp, fine needles kept poking through the yarn itself and splitting it. I decided that not many people had access to a handspun yarn that fine, and fewer still would want to knit that finely, including me. So I went for a looser tension (10½ sts = 1 in, or 16 sts = 4cm), the same yarn and larger (Size 1) needles.

If the tension and the small needle size frighten you, remember that ribbing comes out larger than stockinette stitch on the same size needles, and try knitting one of the smaller sizes for someone you care about, or for yourself!

For the intermediate knitter.

Sizes: Child's 8–10 (women's small, women's medium, men's medium, men's large).

Yarn: 1590 yd/lb (3197 m/kg), 14 wraps/in (22/4 cm). Robin used Brunswick Yarns Pomfret, a softly spun sport weight yarn.

Gauge: Over k 2, p 1 ribbing, 10½ sts = 1 in (16 sts = 4 cm). To count, pull the knit apart widthwise just enough to be able to see the crack where the single purl stitch is in each group of stitches because the purl rib will be stretched apart slightly by the shag added later.

Needles: One set of dpn, size 1 (2.5 mm, 12) or size to reach gauge given above; one dpn, size 4 (3.5 mm, 9); blunt yarn needle.

Instructions: Cuff: Cast 57 (63, 72, 84, 93) sts onto 3 smaller dpn, using the twisted loop cast on (page 12). Divide sts so that there are the same number on each needle, and each needle starts with the first k st of a rib. K 2, p 1 straight up for 3 (3, 3, 3, 3) in.

Thumb gore: For right mitten, start thumb gore in the first rib of the first needle of the rnd. Sl the last p st of the rnd onto the first needle. P this, k 1. Lift and twist the loop between sts, and k it. K 1, p 1. The two outside p sts mark the edges of the thumb gore. Inc in the st next to them, maintaining the ribbing pattern, adding 2 new sts every 4th rnd until there are 13 (13, 19, 19, 25) sts within (not including) the two marking sts.

The effect on the original mitten is of the p incs branching off from the column of marking p sts, so you will sometimes be increasing in the first marking st and in the 1st k st before the second marking st, at other times in the rib itself. The ribs should appear to be rising straight up, with new ribs arising from the marking sts.

Continue ribbing straight up until thumb gore is 2½ (2½, 3, 3, 3½) in (6, 6, 7½, 7½, 9 cm) long measured along the edge of the increase. Take the thumb gore sts, including the p sts, off onto a piece of string or yarn holder, cast on 7 sts over the gap and continue k 2, p 1 ribbing until the total length is 9½ (10, 10½, 10½, 11) in (24, 25, 27, 27, 28 cm) or until just the tips of the ring and forefinger show when the mitten is tried on.

Dec both ends of all 3 needles 1 st from the ends: Rearrange sts so there is an

(continued on page 108)

KENNEBUNK WOOLY BEAR MITTENS

equal number on each needle. Then on each needle, k 2, sl 1, k 1 psso. K to 2 sts from end, p 2 tog (if you can; if you can't, k 1, sl the p st, sl both sts back onto left needle and psso) until only 12–14 sts remain. Break yarn leaving a 6 in (15 cm) tail. Using tapestry needle, draw up the remaining sts firmly, then darn back and forth over the tip to reinforce it. Total length should be 10 (10, 11, 11, 11½) in (25, 27, 28, 28, 29 cm).

Thumb: Carefully pick up sts from holder and sts from top of thumb hole so that the rib pattern will continue without a break. Pick up 2 additional sts on inside corner of thumb gore. In the next rnd, maintaining the rib pattern on the front and back of the thumb, dec at the corners to make the rib come out even. K 2, p 1 straight up for 2 (2, 2½, 2½, 3) in (5, 5, 6, 6, 7½ cm), or until just the tip of the thumb shows when the mitten is tried on. Dec as at the fingertips, every round until only 6–9 sts remain. Break yarn, leaving a 6 in (15 cm) tail. Using a tapestry needle, thread the tail through the rem sts and pull them up firmly. Darn back and forth over the tip to secure the tail invisibly.

Turn the mitten inside out and darn in all tails before shagging the inside. Make the second mitten before shagging the first, lest you lose heart, or forget the measurements. Shagging changes the size of the mitten slightly, making it a little wider and longer. Put the thumb gore on the end of the last needle instead of the beginning of the first, although it really makes little difference, as the 3-way decrease makes the mitten suitable for either hand.

TO SHAG this mitten, turn the completed mitten inside out. The appearance from the inside is of a k 1, p 2 ribbing. Looped shag is applied to the k 1 rib, simply whipped through each st of each k rib working from cuff edge to finger tip. There are no knots, no fancy sts; the yarn is simply overhand-stitched through the rib around a size 4 knitting needle used as a spacer. The tightness of the knit and the fluffiness and roughness of the wool will hold it in place for a hundred years.

Start shagging at edge of cuff, using a blunt tapestry needle and a double strand of yarn. (A contrasting color used for the shagging will show through a little on the outside—a nice effect if it suits you.) Draw the double strand through one k st (from right to left) until there is only about an inch of tail. Lay the size 4 needle on the k rib and draw the yarn through the next k st in the rib so that the yarn wraps around the knitting needle as you stitch. Continue to stitch through one k st after the other, over the knitting needle, to form a series of loops like a wooly caterpillar moving up the rib. Follow the rib to its end, not moving to another rib when it runs out.

Leave the tails, as they're easier to hold out of the way when they're a little long. When you simply have to try the mitten on, prune some out of your way, and when you're all finished, trim them to the same height as the loops. Don't worry about securing the ends. They'll take care of themselves.

Repeat this for all 24 k ribs. Do the thumb gore separately, and start the line of shagging for the inside of the thumb at the tip of the thumb, shag down the thumb, then up the line of the index finger portion of the mitten.

I found it easiest to hold the mitten in my left hand, looking straight down the knitting needle at the next k st and bending the top of the mitten away from me to "open" the st.

Although I thought the shagging would take a long time, when I checked the clock, it took an average of 15 minutes per rib. This meant that I spent about the same amount of time shagging as ribbing, and the reward for finishing was a wonderfully warm mitten.

Reversible Two-Faced Mittens

Carol Thilenius

A GIFT PAIR of red and white Scandinavian mittens from a favorite aunt is a special childhood memory for Carol Thilenius of Juneau, Alaska. "The charm of the Scandinavian patterns lasted far longer than the mittens," she writes, "and encouraged me to try various two-color patterns when I learned to knit."

Carol learned to apply the technique of reversible two-faced knitting to her color patterning in order to improve tension control and avoid long loops on the back. This technique gives a smooth stockinette surface on both sides with the pattern colors reversed. Carol found basic directions for this technique in *Scandinavian Snow Sets* by Kajsa Lindquist.

In addition to her knitting and spinning, Carol is an accomplished weaver, holding the Handweavers Guild of America's Certificate of Excellence. She teaches rug and tapestry weaving in Juneau.

For the expert knitter.

Size: Adult medium.

Yarn: 1700 yd/lb (3400 m/kg), 18 wraps/in (28/4 cm). Carol used a fine 2-ply handspun, similar in weight to a fingering yarn. She used 2 oz (56 g) of natural black and 1 oz (28 g) white.

Gauge: Counting sts of a single layer only, 6–7 sts = 1 in (9–11 sts = 4 cm).

Needles: One set of dpn, size 1 (2.5 mm, 12) or size to reach gauge given above.

Instructions: With cuff color cast on 50 sts loosely over two needles. Remove one needle. Divide sts on three needles and join. Work in rnds of k 1, p 1 rib for 4 in (10 cm).

Next rnd: K 1, p 1 in each st around thus doubling the number of sts. The k sts will form one side and the p sts form the opposite side.

To beg the pattern, read the diagram from right to left for one mitten and left to right for the other. Work the pattern in the *knit* sts as you wish it to appear on the side facing you and follow each k st with a p st of the opposite color. Be sure both yarns are in the back when you knit and that both yarns are in the front when you purl. This results in the yarn not in use being carried between the two layers.

For example, starting at the right edge of the chart, the first square is dark, so work the first k st with dark yarn, throw both yarns to the front, purl the first purl st with the light yarn and throw both yarns to the back. Each pattern square represents one k st for the layer facing you and one p st in the opposite color for the opposite side. The next five squares are light so k the next k st with light, throw both yarns to the front, p with dark and throw both to the back; repeat for the next four pairs of sts. The first few rows are the most difficult since the pattern is not apparent until several rows have been knitted. Don't give up! Just be sure you are alternating k and p sts, throwing both yarns across between sts and following each k st with a p st of the opposite color.

Start the thumb gusset in the 8th rnd by inc one pair of sts after the first thumb outline st and before the last thumb outline st. The increases are made by knitting in the st below the next k st, and purling in the st below the next p st, before knitting and purling the sts themselves. Continue following the graphed pattern, increasing on the thumb gusset every third rnd as shown through the 19th rnd. Sl the 26 sts for the thumb (including the outline sts) to a st holder. Cast on 10 sts as shown in the 20th rnd; one pair dark-light, 3 pairs light-dark and one pair dark-light.

Follow the diagram until you are ready to decrease for the tip. Decreases are done every round on both sides of the edge outline.

To decrease, knit two stitches together while holding the intervening purl st on a holder, then purling the two purl sts together.

Continue to dec to the end of the pattern diagram where 36 sts will remain. Put the k sts for the palm side on one needle, the p sts on a holding string; the k sts for the back-of-the-hand on a second needle and the p sts on the holding string. Tuck the holding string inside and weave the palm and back-of-the-hand knit sts tog as you would the toe of a sock (kitchener stitch, page 39) using the color of the edge outline. This will carry the edge outline across the tip of the mitten. Turn the mitten inside out, put the sts from the holding string on needles, and weave them together with the other color.

For the thumb, pick up the 26 sts on two needles and pick up 18 sts at the inside of the thumb on a third needle. Work in rnds following the pattern. Dec and weave the end as on the main part of the mitten.

Insert hands in mittens and enjoy!

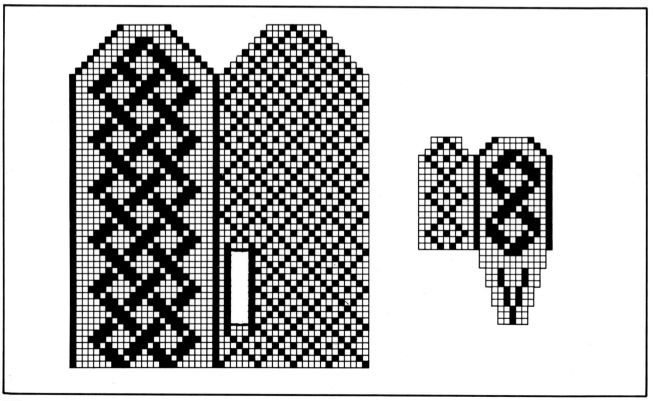

REVERSIBLE TWO-FACED MITTENS

Two-End Mittens, *Carol Rhoades*

"THESE MITTENS," Carol Rhoades says, "combine all the things I like to have in a mitten—double stranding for warmth, side thumb gussets, and a top shaping that avoids those little spaces that you get when you use the usual skp, k 2 tog decrease."

Carol's mittens are worked in a technique called *tvåändstickning* in Swedish. The subtle ribbed surface occurs when one of the two strands is held under slightly tighter tension. A nice variation would be to use two contrasting colors. As a variation, Carol suggests using a single strand and regular stockinette stitch, substituting three inches of k 3, p 1 ribbing for her purl twist patterns.

For the experienced knitter.

Size: Women's medium.

Yarn: 1200 yd/lb (2400 m/kg), 12 wraps/in (19/4 cm). Carol used about 210 yd (192 m) of softly spun 3-ply Corriedale, similar in weight to a sport yarn.

Gauge: 9 sts = 1 in (14 sts = 4 cm).

Needles: One set of dpn, size 3 (3.25 mm, 10) or size to reach gauge given above.

Instructions: Read Meg Swansen's notes on 2-end knitting on page 70 for a general discussion of this technique. Cast on 54 sts; join.

Work 2 rnds st st, alternating strands as you go.

Work 2 rnds twisted braid as follows: With both strands in front of work, purl around, alternating strands and picking up new strand from on top of old strand.

Work 3 rnds st st.

Work 6 rnds double purl as follows: With one strand in back and one in front, * k 1 with strand in back, p 1 with strand in front; rep from * around.

Work 8 rnds st st.

Thumb gusset: Place marker, inc 1 in first st of rnd by knitting st with both strands of yarn, k 1, inc in next st, place marker; complete rnd in 2-end knitting. On following rnd, each strand of inc is k separately. Inc in this way in st after first marker and before second marker every 4th rnd until there are 17 sts bet markers for thumb. Work 1 rnd, slipping these 17 sts to holder, cast on 3 sts over gap and work even on 54 sts for 4 in (10 cm) more.

Top dec: At each side of mitten mark center 3 sts. Dec by k 2 tog on each side of these 3 sts every rnd until 10 sts rem. Run thread ends through these sts and weave in ends.

Thumb: Move 17 sts from holder to needle and pick up 7 sts more around thumb opening—24 sts. Work even for 2 in (5 cm).

Dec: Rnd 1: (K 2, k 2 tog) around—18 sts.

> **Rnd 2:** Work even.
>
> **Rnd 3:** (K 1, k 2 tog) around—12 sts.
>
> **Rnd 4:** Work even.
>
> **Rnd 5:** K 2 tog around—6 sts.

Fasten off as at mitten top.

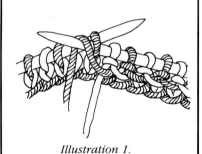
Cathedral Mittens, *Lizbeth Upitis*

WELL-KNOWN as the author of *Latvian Mittens*, a record of and tribute to the finely patterned and meticulously crafted knitwear of her husband's forebears, Lizbeth Upitis of Minneapolis, Minnesota, created this pair of mittens as an elaboration of a pattern knit by her good friend and mentor, Anna Mizena.

"The colors and technique remind me of cathedral windows," she writes, "so I chose sun and morning star symbols to circle the cuff and give light to the windows of the hand." Slip stitches make a warm, colorful mitten that looks more complicated than the one or two colors that are actually used in each row.

Lizbeth is a frequent contributor to *Knitters* magazine, with designs often focusing on very fine knitting and ethnic explorations.

For the intermediate knitter.

Size: Woman's medium.

Yarn: 1500 yd/lb (3000 m/kg), 22 wraps/in (34/4 cm). Lizbeth used a fine, firmly spun 2-ply, Takana from Helmi Vuorelma Oy of Finland. This yarn is usually used for weaving, and gives good stitch definition in this pattern. She used half of a 100-g (3½ oz) skein of black, gold, red, red-orange, purple, and blue.

Gauge: In hand pattern 12 sts = 1 in (19 sts = 4 cm); 12 rows = 1 in (19 rows = 4 cm).

Needles: One set of *five* dpn, size 0 (2.25 mm, 13) or size to reach gauge given above.

Instructions: Right mitten: Cuff: Holding gold and black tog, form sl knot on needle. Using one-needle cast-on (page 12) with gold around thumb and black around index finger, cast on 84 sts not counting sl knot (sts are knit with black; gold forms border). Take slip knot from needle and pull to unfasten. Divide sts evenly on 4 needles. Be certain there is no twist in cast-on row. Cast-on is shown on chart as Rnd 1.

Rnd 2: * K 1 purple, k 1 black; rep from * around.

Rnd 3: Bring both colors forward to purl and keep in front of work. * P 1 purple, pick up black *over* purple and p 1 black; rep from * around (see illustration 1). Be sure to alternate colors, bringing next color *over* last color. Yarn will twist and ply as this rnd is worked, so pull loose approximately 2 yds (2 m) before beginning and push twist away from work.

Rnd 4: With yarns still in front of work, * p 1 purple, p 1 black; rep from * around but bring each color *under* the last as you work around. This untwists the yarn and releases the tangle. Continue with Rnds 5-36 from chart.

Hand pattern: "Window colors" as given in following instructions and on chart are used in following sequence: **Rnds 3, 4, and 5:** red-orange; **Rnds 9, 10 and 11:** blue; **repeat of Rnds 3, 4, and 5:** red; **repeat of Rnds 9, 10 and 11:** purple. Keep to this sequence throughout mitten.

    Rnd 1: With black, k around.

    Rnd 2: With black, p around.

→ 1 rep of palm pattern

□ black
Ⓥ purl black
⊡ gold
⊠ red
◣ red-orange
■ purple
ⓞ window color
◪ slip stitch

Rnds 3, 4 and 5: K 1 window color, k 1 gold, * sl 2, k 1 gold, k 2 window color, k 1 gold; rep from * until 4 sts rem, sl 2, k 1 gold, k 1 window color.

Rnd 6: K 2 gold, * sl 2, k 4 gold; rep from * until 4 sts rem, sl 2, k 2 gold.

Rnds 7 and 8: Rep Rnds 1 and 2.

Rnds 9, 10 and 11: Sl 1, * k 1 gold, k 2 window color, k 1 gold, sl 2; rep from * ending final rep with sl 1 instead of sl 2.

Rnd 12: Sl 1, * k 4 gold, sl 2; rep from * ending with sl 1 instead of sl 2. Rep these 12 rows following window color sequence as indicated above.

At the same time, while keeping to hand pat as established, when 31 rnds of hand pat have been completed, begin right thumb opening.

Right thumb: Keeping to hand pat as established, work hand pat Rnd 2 across first two needles (back of hand); on third needle, work 1 st, cast on 18 sts by making backward lps on right needle (see M 1, page 13). Sl next 18 sts from third needle onto contrasting thread. Be certain there is no twist in cast-on sts. Work last 2 sts of third needle; complete rnd.

Continue in hand pat as established, until 84 rnds of hand pat are completed or to required length. Stretch mitten when measuring, as it will be stretched in blocking. Work Rnds 1 and 2 of hand pat st.

Finger tip shaping: * Knit 1 in black, with gold SSK, work across needles 1 and 2 in pat as established to last 2 sts, k 2 tog with gold; rep from * for needles 3 and 4.

Continue in pat while dec 2 sts each side of hand for a total of 4 sts dec each rnd. When 8 sts remain * k 1 black, sl 1, k 2 tog with gold, psso; rep from *—4 sts rem. Draw gold and black through rem sts, secure and pull to wrong side. Weave in all ends on wrong side.

Thumb: Transfer 18 sts from holding thread to 2 needles. Pick up 18 cast-on sts on 2 needles for back of thumb. Pick up and twist 1 st on the outer end of each needle at thumb corners for ease—40 sts. Purl 1 rnd with black. Work 1 rnd to continue pat of front of thumb.

Next rnd: K 2 tog at beg of first and third needles—38 sts.

Following rnd: SSK last 2 sts of needles 2 and 4.

Continue thumb on rem 36 sts in hand pat until ready to begin black rows after 2nd blue window on thumb. Dec and finish top of thumb as for finger tip shaping. Sew all ends on wrong side.

Left mitten: Work as for right mitten until thumb opening. Work across first needle in hand pat as established. On second needle, p 2, cast on 18 sts, sl next 18 sts from 2nd needle to holder, p rem sts. Work and dec thumb to match right mitten.

To block, place wet cloth over mitten and press with iron. Dampen and press both sides, then stretch lengthwise to accentuate window. Align start/finish line and top decs and press again. Rep until mitten is correct length. Enjoy your craftsmanship

Good Basic Gloves, *Rita Buchanan*

GOOD GLOVES fit well and stay in shape, but given that the human hand is a complex structure, knitting gloves that are both comfortable and functional is a bit of a challenge. Rita Buchanan has mastered the craft by reading and re-reading the section on gloves in Mary Thomas' *Knitting Book*, by looking at old gloves in museum collections and new gloves in stores, and by measuring a lot of hands!

Rita's advice to beginning glove knitters: "Be sure your gauge is exactly right, stick to simple stitch patterns (no Fair Isles or Arans until you've made a few pairs in stockinette or seed stitch), and do a careful job of tucking in all loose yarn ends when you're done knitting."

Rita's favorite gloves so far have been knitted from her own highly elastic handspun yarns, about the weight of commercial sport yarns. Her spinning, knitting, and weaving skills are well known to readers of *Spin·Off* magazine, which she contributes to regularly. She is author of *A Weaver's Garden* (Interweave Press, 1987), and an editor of *Fine Gardening* magazine. Rita and her husband Steve live in Connecticut.

For the intermediate knitter.

Size: Adult small/medium. Changes for large/extra large are given in parentheses. The smaller size will fit *around* most women's hands, the larger *around* most men's. Adjust finger length to suit the wearer.

Yarn: 1500 yd/lb (3015 m/kg), 15 wraps/in (23/4 cm). Rita used 2 to 3 oz (57–85 g) 2-ply handspun Corriedale for the brown gloves, and commercially-spun wool sport-weight yarn for the red gloves.

Gauge: This pattern can be used to make gloves for teenagers or adults in Sizes Small, Medium, Large and Extra Large, depending on the gauge. This is very important: Measure gauge over a large swatch before casting on for gloves! You can get a smaller gauge and knit smaller gloves by using finer yarn, smaller needles, or stockinette stitch. Knit larger gloves with the same or thicker yarn on larger needles or in one of pattern stitches given below.

Over st used for hand part of glove:
    Size Small: 15 sts = 2 in (12 sts = 4 cm)
    Size Medium: 14 sts = 2 in (11 sts = 4 cm)
    Size Large: 13 sts = 2 in (10 sts = 4 cm)
    Size Extra Large: 12 sts = 2 in (9½ sts = 4 cm)

Needles: One set of dpn, size 0 (2.25 mm, 13), size 1 (2.5 mm, 12), or size 2 (2.75–3 mm, 11)—select size to reach gauge given above; one set of dpn a size smaller.

Sl st pat used on red gloves:
    Rnd 1: Knit.
    Rnd 2: (Sl 1 as to k, with yarn in back, k 3) across.

Textured pattern used on brown gloves (worked over an even number of sts):
    Rnd 1: Knit.
    Rnd 2: K 1, p 1.
    Rnd 3: Knit.
    Rnd 4: P 1, k 1.

See how little finger fits here

Right Glove

See how thumb is offset toward palm

A simple ridged pattern, also suitable for gloves (worked over an even number of sts):

> **Rnds 1 and 2:** Knit.
> **Rnd 3:** K 1, p 1.

Cuff: Cast on 54 sts; divide on 3 needles. Remember that you will use the yarn tail to mark the beginning and end of rnds. With smaller needles, work in k 1, p 1 rib for 2½ (3) in (6-8 cm).

Left hand: Change to larger needles and work 3 rnds of st st or pat st. If pat st is used, center it on back of hand only (first half of rnd) and continue until division of sts for fingers.

Thumb gusset: First inc rnd: Place marker (redistribute sts to keep marker on needle) inc 1, k 1, inc 1, place second marker on needle; knit rest of rnd—56 sts. Knit 2 (3) rnds.

Second inc rnd: Inc in first st after first marker and in last st before second marker; knit rest of rnd. Knit 2 (3) rnds. Continue to inc in this way every 3rd (4th) rnd until there are 19 sts bet beg of rnd and marker (70 sts in all). Knit 3 rnds more.

Set thumb sts aside: Thread a large blunt needle with cotton string and draw it through the 19 sts between markers for thumb, removing markers. Tie string ends tog to set aside the thumb sts. Cast on 3 sts above the thumb opening for the hand, place marker on needle to established new beg of rnd and continue knitting around 54 sts until 3¾ (4¼) in (8-11 cm) above cuff.

Set little finger sts aside: From the marker, k 20 sts, put next 13 sts on a string holder, cast on 3 sts and continue knitting back to marker—44 sts. K 3 rnds.

First (index) finger: From marker, k 7, sl next 29 sts on string holder, cast on 3 sts and k rem 8 sts. Divide these 18 sts on 3 needles and k until finger is 2½ (3) in (6-8 cm) or to fit. You can try glove on, carefully, to see when each finger is long enough. To finish this and all other fingers: k 2 tog around; draw end of yarn through the sts twice and tuck the end in securely.

Second finger: Carefully pull out the string holding the sts and replace 7 sts from back and 7 sts from palm onto needles. Join yarn to glove and pick up 3 sts over cast-on sts beside first finger, k across 7 sts from back of glove, cast on 3 sts and k 7 sts from palm. Divide these 20 sts on 3 needles and knit around until second finger is 2¾ (3¼) in (7-8 cm) or to fit. Finish end.

Ring finger: Pick up 3 sts over cast-on sts beside second finger. Thread rem sts from string holder onto needles and k around 18 sts for 2½ (3) in (6-8 cm) or to fit. Finish end.

Little finger: Pick up 3 sts over cast-on sts beside ring finger. Thread 13 sts from string holder onto needles and knit around these 16 sts for 1¾ (2¼) in (4-6 cm) or to fit. Finish end.

Thumb: Pick up 3 sts over cast-on st beside hand. Thread 19 sts from string holder onto needles and k around these 22 sts for 3 rnds. Dec 1 st over picked up sts—21 sts. K 3 rnds and dec 1 st again—20 sts. Continue on 20 sts until thumb is 2¼ (2¾) in (6-7 cm) or to fit. Finish end.

Right glove: Knit as for left glove up to thumb opening, centering pat st, if used, on last half of rnd. Set aside thumb sts, then put marker on needle *before* casting on 3 sts for hand. To set little finger aside, k 21 sts past marker, put 13 sts on string holder, cast on 3 sts and continue back to marker. K 3 rnds. For first finger, k 8 sts, put 29 sts on string holder, cast on 3 sts and k rem 7 sts back to marker. Make second and third fingers to match left glove.

Finishing: Darn in loose yarn ends, using them to reinforce weak spots at the intersections bet fingers if desired. It's hard to get those cast-on sts and picked up sts to come together just right, especially on your first pair of gloves, so don't hesitate to draw in any loose sts or holes if needed. Wash your gloves in warm soapy water to even out the tension, make all sts look uniform and soften the texture. Rinse well, squeeze out extra moisture in a towel, and spread flat to dry.

Zig-Zag Gloves, *Betty Amos*

MY GREAT-GRANDMOTHER taught me the rudiments of knitting," Betty Amos writes; "And as I am now a great-grandmother myself, that was truly back in the historic past. At that time, I remember knitting numerous dish cloths and pot holders, all in garter stitch. Production of these items seemed to be synchronized with periods of bad weather, and I have a feeling that getting me to knit was a desperate measure to keep me quiet during periods when I couldn't be sent outdoors to play. At any rate, once I grew older, all it took to keep me quiet was a continual supply of good books, so my interest in knitting went on a prolonged 60-year hold."

When Betty combined households with her handspinning son and daughter-in-law, she was captivated by the glorious dyed fleeces that seemed to be everywhere, and the urge to knit resurfaced. Subtle hints that she'd love for one of them to spin up some knitting yarn for her resulted in the gift of a spinning wheel—she was on her own!

"Eventually," she says, "I learned how to spin knitting yarns that I thoroughly enjoy using. Next, I began to wonder how I was going to use all this new found treasure. Being of mature years and with a figure like a bean, garments of brilliant color and dazzling pattern are not a wise choice for my wardrobe. In any case, large items, such as sweaters, take too long to knit since I'm always impatient to try out new designs and colors. My solution is to concentrate my knitting on small articles of wearing apparel. Scarves, hats, knee socks (see page 149), gloves, and mittens are all short-term knitting projects that can be worn by anyone. They offer unlimited scope for color and design, and there is no danger of having to decorate the walls with the finished items, since they make eagerly accepted gifts."

The bold pattern in Betty's Zig-Zag Gloves was inspired by a pair of mittens by Phyllis Montague of Labrador which appeared in *Fox and Geese*

and Fences *and Fences* by Robin Hansen. The striking pattern, she says, is easy enough for a beginning two-color knitter.

For the intermediate knitter.

Size: Women's medium.

Yarn: 1500 yd/lb (1371 m/kg), 18 wraps/in (28/4 cm). Betty used about 1 oz (28 g) each of natural gray (A) and dyed magenta (B) handspun wool in a firmly-twisted fingering weight.

Gauge: Over stockinette st, 9 sts = 1 in (14 sts = 4 cm).

Needles: One set of *five* dpn, size 0 (2.25 mm, 13), or size to reach gauge given above.

Instructions: With dominant color, A, cast on 60 sts on 4 needles. Divide sts as follows: 12, 16, 16, 16. Join and work in k 2, p 2 rib for 2½ in (6 cm). Change to st st, inc 10 sts evenly spaced around next rnd—70 sts. Begin pat with A, following chart.

Note that thumb gores are started in the first pat row. For left glove, gore begins with sts 11, 12, 13 and 14 on the first needle. For right glove the thumb gore begins with sts 4, 5, 6, and 7 on the 4th needle. All thumb gore sts are worked in solid color with A. The position of the four thumb gore sts are outlined on chart with dotted lines. Of course, work only one thumb gore on each glove.

Shaping thumb gore: Beg with Rnd 3 of pat, inc 1 st in second and in the next to last st of the gore. Inc 2 sts in this way every 3rd rnd until there are 22 sts in the gore; this is at the end of Rnd 27. Work even in pat for 3 rnds more.

Next rnd: For left glove, knit first 10 sts in pat on first needle, sl 22 sts of gore on holders, cast on 4 sts on first needle for a bridge across the gap, and k rem 3 sts in pat on first needle; continue in pat to end of rnd.

Next rnd: Continuing in pat, work all 17 sts of first needle and to end of rnd; work until 44th rnd of chart is completed. Break off color B.

To center the design on back of hand, redistribute sts as follows: For left glove, with A, k first 2 sts of first needle and place marker, k 9, place marker, k 20 sts, place marker, k 9, place marker, k 8, place marker, k 16, place marker, k last 6 sts from 4th needle. Break off yarn. Keeping 20 sts bet 2nd and 3rd markers for index finger on needle, divide rem 50 sts evenly on 2 holders.

The chart at right shows the arrangement of sts at this point and the order in which they are to be worked.

Index finger: With A, cast on 4 sts to form bridge bet palm and back of glove, and k first st of 20 sts of finger. Divide the next 18 sts on 2 (or 3) needles and sl 20th st to end of 4-st bridge. K these 24 sts to desired length for finger.

Decrease as follows:

Rnd 1: (K 1, k 2 tog) around—16 sts.

Rnd 2 and all even numbered rnds: Work even.

Rnd 3: (K 1, k 2 tog) 5 times, k 1—11 sts.

Rnd 5: (K 1, k 2 tog) 3 times, k 2—8 sts.

Rnd 7: (K 1, k 2 tog) twice, k 2—6 sts.

Rnd 9: K 2 tog 3 times—3 sts rem.

On Using Five Needles Instead of Four

American double pointed needles usually come in sets of four, while European ones come in fives. It's worth seeking out sets of five, or even buying two sets and combining them if you knit a lot of small projects in the round. As Betty Amos explains:

The human head has a front, back, and two sides. So does an arm or leg. Hands and feet have upper and lower sides and two edges, and articles designed to fit these shapes often come in four sections. Setting up a four-panel lace pattern or a diagram for two-color knitting on three needles can get pretty complicated, so I take the easy way out and use the number of needles that best fits the design: four for the tube, and one working needle.

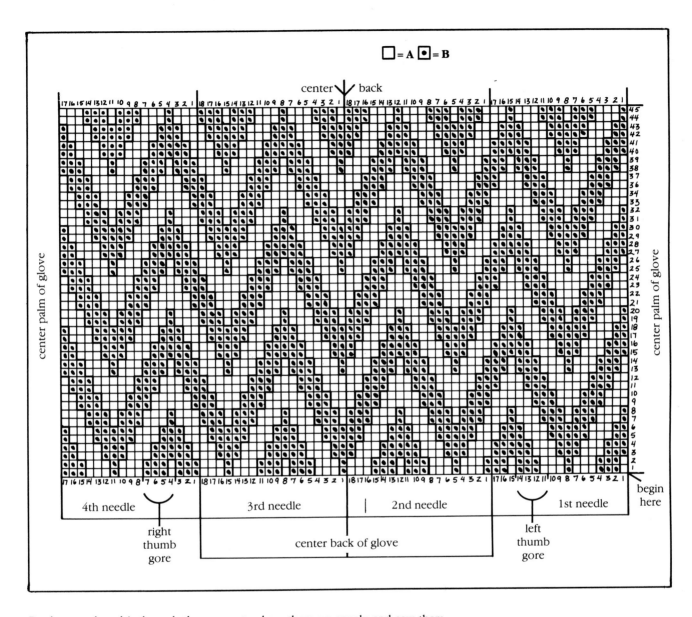

Break yarn, thread it through these rem sts, draw them up snugly and sew them together.

Middle finger: Sl 9 sts from each of palm and back holders to two needles. Pick up 4 sts from bridge at base of index finger on a 3rd needle. Tie in yarn on 4th needle and cast on 4 sts for bridge. Work even on these 26 sts until work measures 1 in (2½ cm) from bridge. Dec 2 sts on next row, continue working on rem 24 sts until finger is desired length. Finish by dec as for index finger.

Ring finger: Sl 8 sts from each of back and palm holder to 2 needles. Pick up 4 sts from bridge at base of previous finger and cast on 4 sts for 2nd bridge as for middle finger; work on these 24 sts to desired length. Finish by dec as for index finger.

Little finger: Sl rem 8 sts from each holder to 2 needles. Pick up 5 sts from bridge at base of ring finger. Work on these 21 sts to desired length.

Dec rnds:

Rnd 1: (K 1, k 2 tog) 7 times—14 sts.

Rnd 2 and all even numbered rnds: Work even.

Rnd 3: (K 1, k 2 tog) 4 times, k 2—10 sts.

Rnd 5: (K 1, k 2 tog) 3 times, k 1—7 sts.

Rnd 7: K 2 tog 3 times, k 1—4 sts.

Break yarn, thread it through these rem sts, draw them up snugly and sew them together.

Thumb: Pick up 4 sts of thumb bridge and sl 22 sts of thumb gore from holders—26 sts. Divide on 3 or 4 needles. Tie in A and work even to desired length.

Dec rnds:

Rnd 1: (K 1, k 2 tog) 8 times, k 2—18 sts.

Rnd 2 and all even numbered rnds: Work even.

Rnd 3: (K 1, k 2 tog) 6 times—12 sts.

Rnd 5: (K 1, k 2 tog) 4 times—8 sts.

Rnd 7: (K 1, k 2 tog) twice, k 2—6 sts. Break yarn, thread it through these rem sts, draw them up snugly and sew them together.

The thumb and fingers of the right glove are worked in the same way except that the position of the fingers is reversed (index finger on same edge as thumb gore) and the 4 sts of the thumb gore begin with sts 4, 5, 6, and 7 on the 4th needle. To finish the gloves, pull all yarn ends to the inside of glove, turn glove and fingers inside out and darn the ends invisibly into the inside sts.

Nova Scotia Snowflake Gloves

Janetta Dexter

LUNENBURG COUNTY, Nova Scotia, where Janetta Dexter grew up, has always been populated by craftspeople. "My mother," she writes, "was a knitter, trained seamstress, quilt maker, and rug hooker. Grandmother, who lived with us, had been a weaver, but had not been able to bring her loom to our small home. She was 72 years old when I was born in 1921, and still made mats, quilts, and knitted mittens for her numerous grandchildren.

"I learned to knit from her, since Mother was left-handed and I found it difficult to follow her directions. She taught me two of the simpler color-stranded patterns. Mother didn't do color patterns, but did socks, sweaters, and gloves in plain and textured stitch patterns. In my teens I learned to do plain gloves from her."

Over the years, as school teacher and later wife and mother of three, Janetta continued to knit, and also learned spinning, weaving, and natural dyeing. After retiring from teaching in 1971, she began collecting color-stranded patterns from elderly ladies whom she met at craft fairs and sheep festivals. In 1971, with the help of her friend Betty Hearn, she arranged these patterns in a booklet which was later published and sold by the Nova Scotia Museum. The snowflake motif in these gloves appears in the most recent edition. She also collaborated with Robin Hansen on *Flying Geese and Partridge Feet* (Down East Books, Camden, Maine).

Here, then, is Janetta's offering: an old Nova Scotian pattern adapted to her mother's glove pattern using her grandmother's two-color knitting technique.

For the intermediate knitter.

Size: Child's large or women's small. Suggestions for men's sizes are given at end.

Yarn: 1590 yd/lb (3197 m/kg), 14 wraps/in (22/4 cm). Janetta used Brunswick Pomfret, a softly spun sport-weight yarn, 2 oz (56 g) of dark yarn and 1½ oz (42 g) of white.

Gauge: With smaller needles over Snowflake pat 9 sts = 1 in (14 sts = 4 cm).

Needles: One set of dpn, size 0 (2.25 mm, 13) or size to reach gauge given above; one set of dpn, size 2 (2.75–3 mm, 11) or two sizes larger than gauge needles.

Instructions: Left glove: With dark yarn and larger needles cast on 63 sts. Divide evenly on 3 needles. Knit off to smaller needles and work in k 2, p 1 ribbing for 2½ in (6 cm).

Next rnd: Change to st st and continue with smaller needles, inc 7 sts—70 sts.
Begin Salt and Pepper pat:

Rnd 1: * dark, 1 light; rep from * around.

Rnd 2: * K 1 light, 1 dark; rep from * around. These 2 rnds establish Salt and Pepper pat.

Rnd 3: Begin Snowflake pat on back of hand as follows: Work first 2 sts in salt and pepper pat, place marker for beg of Snowflake pat, work first row of smaller Snowflake chart over next 31 sts, place marker for end of Snowflake pat, complete row in Salt and Pepper pat as established.

Rnd 4: Begin thumb gusset: Work in Snowflake/Salt and Pepper pats as established to last 7 sts of rnd; place marker for beg of thumb gusset. Keeping to alternating color pat, (inc by knitting into next st with both colors) twice, complete rnd in pat, place marker for end of thumb gusset (this is also rnd of rnd)—72 sts.

Rnds 5, 6 and 7: Continue in pats as established, working inc sts in Salt and Pepper pat.

Rnd 8: Work in pats to last 2 sts of rnd; keeping to alternating color pat, (inc by knitting into next st with both colors) twice—74 sts.

Rnds 9, 10, and 11: Rep Rnd 5.

Rnd 12: Work in pat to first thumb gusset marker, inc in each of next 2 sts as on Rnd 4—76 sts.

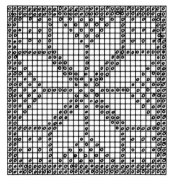

Smaller snowflake

Rnds 13, 14 and 15: Rep Rnd 5.

Rnd 16: Rep Rnd 8—78 sts.

Rnds 17, 18 and 19: Rep Rnd 5.

Rnd 20: Rep Rnd 12—80 sts.

Rnd 21: Rep Rnd 5.

Rnd 22: Work in pats to first thumb gusset marker, remove marker, sl last 17 sts of rnd to holding yarn, remove 2nd thumb marker, cast on 7 sts over gap—70 sts.

Work even in pats until Snowflake chart is completed. Change to Salt and Pepper pat. Work even for 2 rnds.

Little finger: Knit to 9 sts before center of rnd. Sl next 18 sts to holding yarn for little finger; cast on 6 sts over gap—58 sts. K 2 rnds. Adjust sts on needles.

Ring finger: K to 10 sts before center of rnd, sl next 20 sts to holding yarn for ring finger, cast on 6 sts over gap—44 sts. K 1 rnd; adjust sts.

Middle finger: K to 11 sts before center of rnd, sl next 22 sts to holding yarn, cast on 6 sts over gap—28 sts. Adjust sts.

Index finger: Knit rem 28 sts of index finger for 2¾ in (7 cm). Next rnd: [(Sl 1, k 1, psso) 3 times, (k 2 tog) 4 times] twice—14 sts. Rep last rnd—7 sts. Draw yarn through rem sts and pull up tightly.

Middle finger: Pick up 6 sts along lower edge of index finger, being careful not to leave holes at the corners. Place these and the 22 sts from holding yarn on 3 needles—28 sts. K middle finger in pat for 3 in (8 cm); finish as for index finger.

Work 3rd and 4th fingers in the same way, picking up 6 sts at base of previous finger and knitting 2 tog around on last 2 rnds to dec (k odd st at end of rnd when necessary).

I always leave the thumbs until both gloves are otherwise finished, as it facilitates measuring. Pick up 9 sts along 7 cast-on sts of thumb opening; place 17 sts from holding yarn onto needle. Adjust sts and k to required length; dec as for fingers.

When knitting the right glove, reverse position of pats and fingers. To make other sizes: Each inc in size requires 8 more sts at beg of pat area: 4 in palm and 4 in back. These extra sts may be dealt with in several ways:

1. By enlarging the Snowflake motif as in diagram.
2. By enlarging the dark border around Snowflake.
3. By adding the extra sts to the Salt and Pepper surrounding the dark border.

For Size Man's Small, cast on 69 sts on cuff and inc 9 sts rather than 7 in first st st row. Add 2 sts to each finger.

For Size Man's Medium, cast on 75 sts and inc 11 sts in first st st row. Add 4 sts to each finger.

Gloves might also be made larger by using a slightly heavier yarn and larger needle.

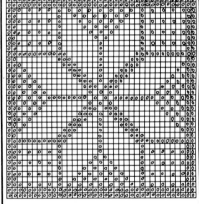

Enlarged snowflake

CUFF TO TIP TWO-NEEDLE GLOVES

Cuff-to-tip Two Needle Gloves

Ginny Norris

Y OU'VE ALREADY MET the wonderful trick of knitting a tubular fabric on only two needles in Ingvor Johnson's mittens (page 74). Ginny Norris of Santa Barbara, California, extends the technique to the complexities of glove construction in this handsome pair which has a dressy doubled cuff and an embroidered rose motif taken from a hooked rug worked by her mother-in-law.

Ginny was taught to knit at the age of nine by her mother. "I sat beside Mother while my sister, who is left-handed, sat in front of her. Betty learned to purl and knit while I learned to knit and purl. Mother never required us to knit just-so, and, since Mom made up her patterns as she knit, we were taught to think up our own ways of doing things. This legacy has led me to always want to do things a little differently—to take ideas from all about and play with them all at once."

Ginny learned to spin in 1962 with Eileen Stace in New Zealand; this skill has sharpened her interest in all aspects of textile craft.

For the expert knitter.

Size: Adult medium. The hemmed cuff is not made like a traditional cuff, but will stretch to fit.

Yarn: 1500 yd/lb (1370 m/kg), 18 wraps/in (28/4 cm). Ginny's yarn is handspun 2-ply natural black Karakul/Corriedale cross in a fingering weight. Her gloves used 2 oz (57 g). She also used small amounts of a similar weight wool in shades of red and green for embroidery, a small amount of "waste" yarn (about the same weight but in a contrasting color), and several yards of "ravel cord" (slippery braided nylon or perle cotton).

Gauge: 7½ sts = 1 in (12 sts = 4 cm).

Needles: Two dpn *each* in size 3 (3.25 mm, 10) or size to reach gauge given above, size 5 (3.75–4 mm, 8), and size 1 (2.5 mm, 12). (Editor's note: This pattern is a prime example of how tubes—even very small tubes like the fingers on a glove—can be worked without seams while working back and forth in rows on two needles. In theory this could be done on single pointed needles, but because this design also involves rearranging the sts on the needles several times to form the double cuff and a few other techniques that require access to both ends of the row of sts, it's simpler to use dpn. Size 5 needles are used for cuff, Size 3 needles for rem of glove; Size 1 needles are used only to transfer and rearrange sts.)

Instructions: Cuff: With Size 5 needles and waste yarn cast on 26 sts. (This is half the number of sts used for the hand of the glove; cuff is worked on a needle two sizes larger than the hand and so will stretch to fit around the wrist.) Break off yarn. Using ravel cord k 1 row. Break off ravel cord. With waste yarn, begin to tubular knit as follows:

Row 1: * With yarn in front, sl 1 as to purl, with yarn in back, knit 1; rep from * across.

Row 2: Rep Row 1. At the end of Row 2 one rnd is completed. Remember: With tubular knitting 2 rows = 1 rnd.

Tubular Knitting On Two Needles

Describing the two-needle tubular knit, Ginny Norris says, "You can amaze yourself and others as you produce a tubular fabric while apparently knitting a flat one. To do so, simply slip one stitch and knit the next in sequence; thus you knit the side facing you while you skip the side away from you. The second row completes the other side of the tube, as you continue with the slip, knit pattern."

With an *even* number of stitches, here's how the pattern would read for both rows in the sequence:
* Yarn forward, sl 1, yarn back, k 1. Repeat from *.

With an odd number of stitches, the two rows start and end differently:
Row 1: *Sl 1, k 1, repeat from * to next to last st. End with an extra k 1.
Row 2: Sl 2, k 1, *sl 1, k 1, repeat to end of row.

Remember that *two rows* make one *round*. As your tube grows, it's a good idea to check periodically to make sure that you haven't missed bringing the yarn forward for a slip stitch (thereby capturing a stitch from the other side), or idly purled a slip stitch (again catching a stitch from the other side). "If you find such a glitch", Ginny says, "simply follow the stitches that form a column above it up to the needle, release the top stitch, and drop it down to free that errant stitch. Then chain the dropped stitches back up again with a latch hook or crochet hook."

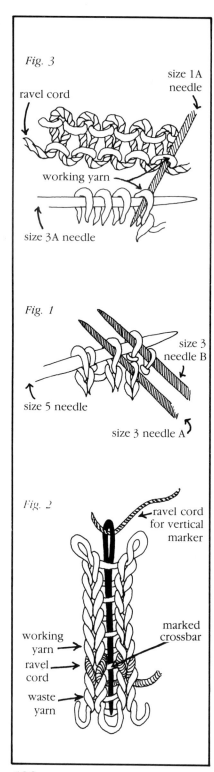

Fig. 3

ravel cord

size 1A needle

working yarn

size 3A needle

Fig. 1

size 3 needle B

size 5 needle

size 3 needle A

Fig. 2

ravel cord for vertical marker

working yarn

ravel cord

waste yarn

marked crossbar

Work 2 more rnds (4 rows more). With ravel cord tubular knit 1 rnd (2 rows). Change to working yarn and leaving a 15 in (38 cm) tail, tubular knit 54 rnds or 2½ times the desired cuff length. Since this is a double cuff you will need twice the desired length; the additional ½ length is to compensate for the length lost when the cuff stretches to fit around the wrist.

After you have completed 3 or 4 rnds, you will begin to see that you are actually knitting a tube! It is a good idea to check periodically to make sure that you haven't missed bringing the yarn forward for a sl st (thereby capturing a st from the other side) or idly purled a sl st (again linking with the other side). If you find such a st simply follow the sts that form a column above it up to the needle, release the top st and drop it down to free that errant st, then chain the dropped sts back up again. A latch hook or crochet hook will speed this task.

Return to the cast-on edge and firmly pull out the ravel cord that joins the cast-on sts to the waste yarn. Open the tube gently and catch all the released waste-yarn lps on a cord and tie in a loose circle. Check for any sts caught in the tube and correct them.

Back at the last rnd worked, transfer the first st (it has the purl side toward you) to a Size 3 needle (we'll refer to this as needle B) that will be in back, and the next st (the knit st) to another Size 3 needle (we'll refer to this as needle A) that will be in front (fig 1). Continue across the Size 5 needle until all slip (purl) sts are on Size 3 B needle in back and all knit sts are on Size 3 A needle in front. Now the top of the tube is open.

Before forming the hem, to prevent the hem from being twisted, baste a ravel cord through the cross bars bet the last st and first st of the rnd. (fig. 2). Mark the final cross bar of the working yarn (just above the ravel cord). Baste a second ravel cord vertically through the cross bars at the midpoint of the rnd (opposite end of the needles).

Fold the cast-on end into the tube and upward until the ravel cord sts are just above the sts on the needles, with the waste yarn extending upward beyond the needles. The sts from the bottom of the cuff (first rnd) will show as purl sts.

Alternate these sts from the first rnd with the sts of the last rnd as follows: * Beginning with the marked st (the last cross bar on the first row of the cuff) transfer a p st to the Size 1 needle (we'll call this Size 1 A needle), then transfer a k st from Size 3 A needle to Size 1 A needle (fig 3). ** Transfer the next p st from the bottom of the cuff to the Size 1 A needle, transfer the next k st from the Size 3 A needle to the Size 1 A needle. Rep from ** across until all sts are removed from the Size 3 A needle. You now have 26 sts on the Size 1 A needle. You have worked over or across to the second vertical ravel cord marker.

Transfer rem sts from first row of cuff alternately with rem sts from last row of cuff to Size 1 B needle. Turn your work. There are now 26 on the Size 1 B needle in back and 26 on the Size 1 A needle in front and folded cuff is formed.

Firmly pull out the ravel cord bet the waste yarn and the working yarn; remove the waste yarn and vertical ravel cord markers at beg and midpoint of rnd.

The next step is the most critical. The sts from the back needle will be alternated with the sts from the front needle as they are transferred to a single Size 3 needle as follows: With the Size 1 B needle in back and the Size 1 A needle in front and beg at right end of needles, transfer the first st on the back needle to a Size 3 needle, then transfer the first st on the front needle to the same Size 3 needle; * transfer the next st on the back needle to the same Size 3 needle, transfer the next st on the front needle to the same Size 3 needle. Rep from * across until all sts are transferred from both Size 1 needles to a single Size 3 needle. You now have 52 sts on the Size 3 needle and are ready to begin the hand part of the glove.

Using Size 3 needles, work in tubular knit for 34 rounds or until you reach the base of the little finger; you will make the thumb opening later. Correct any errant sts.

Little finger: On Size 3 needles tubular knit 13 sts. Sl remaining 39 sts on holder. Make a backward lp on right needle to inc 1 st—14 sts. Complete the second row of this round.

Tubular knit 15 rounds (or the length of the little finger, plus one round). Break yarn, leaving an 8 in (20 cm) tail. Remove the needle from the sts, and correct any caught sts. Thread tail through this circle of sts, pull tightly closed and weave in tail.

Return to remaining 39 sts, pick up 1 st from the inc st at the base of the little finger to give 40 sts. Tubular knit 3 rnds.

Ring finger: Tubular knit 14 sts next to the little finger; put rem 26 sts on holder. Work 14 sts for 22 rnds or to the desired length plus one rnd. Correct any errant sts, tie off and finish as before.

Index finger: Sl 14 sts from end of holder farthest from ring finger to needles; tubular for 22 rnds (or index finger measure plus one rnd) and complete as other fingers.

Middle finger: Holding work with little finger at the right, pick up 1 st at base of ring finger; transfer rem 12 sts on holder to needle. Pick up another st at base of the index finger, giving a total of 14 sts. Tubular knit 28 rnds (or middle finger measure plus one rnd) as follows: * K 1, sl 1 with yarn in front; rep from * across. Rep this row for pat to desired length plus 1 rnd. Complete as for other fingers.

Thumb opening: Count 18 rnds up from the wrist into the palm of the hand (or measure from wrist to big knuckle of the thumb). Count 7 palm sts in from the edge of the hand that is in line with the index finger, and break the yarn. Toward that same edge, withdraw the yarn, st by st, catching each lp alternately (from above and below opening) with a Size 1 needle. Stop one st short of the edge st, being sure last lp is above opening (p st). Return to the break and pick up alternate sts as you withdraw the yarn until there are 24 lps collected on the needle being sure last lp caught is below opening (k st). Form a backward lp with each tail of the broken yarn and weave in the tail, giving 26 sts. With Size 3 needles, tubular knit as for hand for one rnd, starting on the side toward the cuff.

Reduce 2 sts at the end of the next 2 rows as follows: At 2 sts short of the end of the row, transfer the completed third-from-the-end st back to left needle. Sl the next-to-the-last st and the last st over this st, then transfer this double dec st to the right needle. At the end of the rnd there are 22 sts.

Tubular knit one rnd. On next rnd make a double dec only on the palm side of the thumb—20 sts. Continue to make double decs on the palm side every other round until 14 sts rem. Continue to tubular knit until thumb is the correct length. Correct any mischievous sts in the thumb tube and finish off like other fingers. Weave in any loose tails and you have finished the first glove! Try it on—admire your work!

Second glove: Work exactly as the first until ready to make the thumb.

Hand In Glove

Here are the measurements that will guarantee you a perfectly fitting glove. Make a gauge sample, and note stitches per inch and rows per inch. Take each measurement carefully, and then convert by multiplying times stitches per inch for circumference measures, or times rows per inch for lengthwise measures. Keep track of your vertical measures in inches on the first glove, and then count rows for its mate.
—Around a finger at its thickest
—Cuff length of choice (2-3 in)
—Wrist to base of little finger
—Base of little finger to tip
—Wrist to base of middle finger
—Base of ring finger to tip
—Base of middle finger to tip
—Base of index finger to tip
—Wrist to big knuckle of thumb
—Big knuckle of thumb to tip

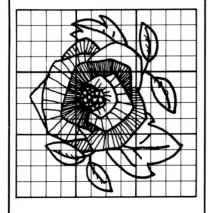

Make the thumb according to the instructions but be sure it is located on the opposite side of the glove so you don't make two left gloves.

Embroidery: Trace rose pattern on tear-away interfacing. Flip design over and trace mirror image of rose on second piece of interfacing. Layer net square, back of glove and interfacing in embroidery hoop. Work various shade of red indicated in drawing in satin stitch. Two different colors are used for the 12 French knots in the center. The finished rose reflected in a mirror makes it easier to embroider the second glove. Tear away interfacing and tweeze out bits caught in the design. Trim off net inside.

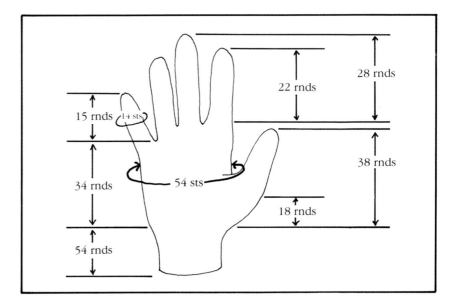

Tip-to-cuff Two Needle Gloves
Beverly Royce

BEVERLY ROYCE has been the guru of two-needle tubular knitting in this country for years. While the technique was known previously in the Scandinavian countries, Beverly figured it out all by herself at her farm home in Langdon, Kansas.

Beverly's self-published booklet, "Notes on Double Knitting", has been an underground sensation among adventurous knitters ever since its publication in 1981. Its instructions for color patterning, circular tams, lined mittens, socks, and more, all knitted on two needles, challenge the imagination.

The gloves shown here are unconventional in construction; you knit all the fingers from the tips down on two needles, and then join them in one round. This allows each finger to have a naturally closed tip, rather than a gathered one that might not wear as well. It eliminates the need to separate into groups those stitches from which the fingers are to be built, or to cast on additional stitches between fingers. The fingers and first few rounds of the hand are worked inside out, which eliminates the drawing in that so often accompanies color-stranded knitting.

After working the fingers and top of hand, Beverly transferred her stitches to a set of double-pointed needles and worked the rest of the glove in the round. "So I could see how the pattern was progressing, and check the fit," she says. You could continue to work on two needles, though.

Beverly is well-known among spinners, too, for her exceptional knitting yarns in fine wools and unusual fiber blends. She holds several "Spin·Off Book of World Records" awards for her handspun, handknitted creations.

For the expert knitter.

Size: Women's medium.

Yarn: 1250 yd/lb (2512 m/kg), 12 wraps/in (19/4 cm). Beverly's yarn is a very lofty 2-ply handspun, similar in weight to a sport yarn. The gloves require about 2 oz (57 g) of light and dark yarn.

Gauge: Over stockinette st, 6½ sts = 1 in (10 sts = 4 cm).

Needles: One set of five dpn, size 4 (3.5 mm), 7 or 8 in (18–20 cm) long, or size to reach gauge given above; 1 set of four dpn two or three sizes smaller for moving and re-arranging sts.

Misc: Eight point protectors; one 10-in (25 cm) single-pointed needle Size 4 (3.5 mm) or smaller for holding fingers.

Instructions: (Editor's note: Double knitting produces a seamless tube while working back and forth in rows. This particular glove design begins at the fingertips and works down, working the tubes inside out until the fingers are joined to the hand. This will prevent carried yarn from pulling too tightly as sometimes happens when tubes are worked right-side out.)

Double knitting is worked as follows over an even number of sts:

Row 1: * Sl 1 purlwise with yarn in back, k 1; rep from * across.

Row 2: Rep Row 1. At the end of Row 2 you have completed the first rnd. In double knitting 2 *rows = 1 rnd.*

Left glove: Begin with the little finger, casting on 14 sts with the dark yarn. Work the first 3 rnds (6 rows). Next shift the stitches as follows: Divide the two layers of the tube onto 2 small size needles, transferring the sl sts to the front needle and the k sts to the back needle. The tube is now open at the top. Next, transfer 4 sts from the end of the front needle to the back needle. Then transfer 4 sts from the other end of the back needle to the front needle. This sounds like busy work, but try it—it makes for very nice finger tips.

Replace the sts back to one needle, alternately, making sure that the first st on the needle is a sl st. This leaves a partially worked row with the working yarn in the middle of the row. Sl the worked sts to the working needle and finish the row with dark yarn.

Top

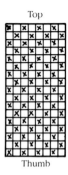

Thumb

Top

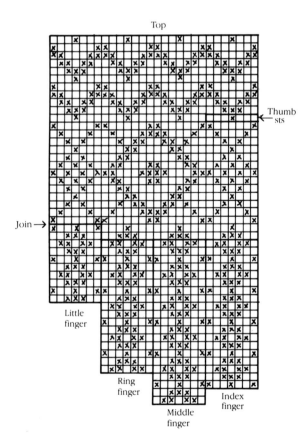

Begin to work pat from chart beginning at the bottom and working up, reading rows from right to left. Chart shows only k sts, so for Row 1 work only the k sts of the first row as shown on the chart. For Row 2, repeat the same row of the chart. At the end of Row 2 one rnd of the finger is completed. Notice that all floats are on the outside of the tube. When you reach the heavy line (10 pat rnds for this finger), break off yarn leaving an 8 in (20 cm) tail. Sl the finger sts to the holding needle, with tail to the left. Weave in yarn end at finger tip.

Repeat for the 3 rem fingers, following their respective charts for the pattern st. When index finger is complete do not break off yarn, just slide it to the holding needle, with working yarn in position to begin a new rnd. Now work the next chart line across first 3 fingers only as shown on chart. Do not follow the line into the little finger area. Take care that each chart line is worked twice. Work next rnd over 3 fingers. Next join the little finger as indicated, working from the chart across the entire width of the hand.

When a few rnds have been completed on the hand section you may wish to distribute the sts among 4 needles and turn the glove right-side out, working around with a fifth needle. Place a marker for the beg of the rnd. Continue to work each chart line twice to end of chart.

Thumb: At the same time, when you reach the point where the thumb will be located for left glove, work the indicated thumb sts in a length of contrasting color waste yarn at the beg of the rnd. Sl these sts back to left needle and work them again following the chart line. When chart is completed, turn the glove back to the wrong side; you need not turn the fingers. Use the point protectors to keep hand sts safe while you work the thumb. Remove the waste yarn from the thumb sts. There will be 7 lps above the opening and 8 lps below the opening; sl these open loops on two small needles, then pick up one st more for upper needle—16 sts. Arrange the sts alternately on one needle making sure the first st is a sl st. Work thumb from the chart using the double knitting pat st. (Having the hand sts on 4 needles instead of just 3 allows you to try on the glove to check the fit and length of thumb.) Shift sts so st on one side or the other of center of row becomes first st of row.

Re-close the thumb tube by arranging sts on a single needle and bind off 2 sts at a time.

Use the yarn ends bet fingers and at the base of the thumb to work duplicate sts to fill in loose sts at base of fingers and thumb. Fasten each yarn end securely on the wrong side, weaving in and out along a line as in grafting.

Finish the glove as follows: Work 3 rnds light, 3 rnds dark, then 8 rnds in light color, dec 12 sts evenly spaced on the first of these last 8 rnds. Work 3 rnds more in dark.

Cuff: Work k 1, p 1 ribbing in the light color to required length, then rib 2 rnds dark. Bind off.

Right glove: Work as for left glove, but reverse the thumb placement by working the waste yarn sts on the last 7 sts of rnd.

Thumb
sts

Join →

Little
finger

Ring
finger

Middle
finger

Index
finger

TIP TO CUFF TWO-NEEDLE GLOVES

Family Socks, *Harriet Rosenquist*

HARRIET ROSENQUIST learned to knit these basic socks when she was only ten years old in her native Finland. Her pattern is easily adaptable to different sizes and color patterns. As the mother of four, Harriet gets lots of practice; she knits a couple of pairs for each family member every year, as well as for friends and their children. "It takes about a day to make a pair of small socks," she says.

Her socks are knitted from a plain, firmly spun 100% wool yarn for excellent comfort and wear. For a thicker sock, she recommends choosing a heavier yarn and larger needles, dropping back a size (for example, for a pair of mother-size socks, use the brother-size pattern), adding extra rows for length as necessary.

For the intermediate knitter.

Size: Little Sister (child's medium); see changes for Brother, Mom, and Dad at end of instructions.

Yarn: 1200 yd/lb (2412 m/kg), 14 wraps/in (22/4 cm). Harriet's yarn is a sturdy 2-ply sport yarn.

Gauge: 7 sts = 1 in (11 sts = 4 cm).

Needles: One set of *five* dpn, size 0 (2.25 mm, 13) or size to reach gauge given above.

Instructions: Cast on 40 sts. Divide evenly on 4 needles; join, being careful not to twist sts. These needles are called (starting with beg of rnd): 1, 2, 3 and 4. The free needle is always referred to as the 5th needle.

Cuff: Work in k 1, p 1 rib in following color sequence: 10 rnds pink, 6 beige, 2 pink, 2 light blue, 2 white, 2 beige. Change to st st and beige; work 2 rnds.

Begin heel: Back of heel: Leaving needles 3 and 4 resting (for instep), k 20 sts from needles 1 and 2 onto a single needle. Work these 20 sts in st st for 11 rows more, ending with a p row.

Shape heel:

    Row 1: K 13, sl 1, k 1, psso, (5 sts rem on left needle)—19 sts. Turn.

    Row 2: P 7, p 2 tog, (5 sts rem on left needle)—18 sts. Turn.

    Row 3: K 7, sl 1, k 1, psso (4 sts rem on left needle)—17 sts. Turn.

    Row 4: P 7, p 2 tog, psso (4 sts rem on left needle)—16 sts. Turn.

Continue in this way until total of 8 sts rem on needle at end of Row 12. Break off yarn.

Foot: With right side of back of heel facing, pick up 7 sts along right edge of heel section, work 8 sts from needle, pick up 7 sts along left edge of heel section, work 20 instep sts from holder to needle—42 sts. Continue to work around on all 4 needles working 4 rnds beige and dec 1 st at beg and midpoint of first rnd—40 sts, 10 on each needle.

Work 28 rnds pink.

FAMILY SOCKS

Standard Heel

The most popular way to turn a heel and the one used (in some variation) in all the sock patterns in this book, is the Standard, "French", or "Dutch" heel. It's a little more trouble to keep track of than other methods, but it gives a smooth, comfortable heel that wears well.

After you've knit down to the ankle on your sock, divide your stitches in half, with half on two needles for the instep, and half on one needle for the heel flap. Knit these heel stitches back and forth in stockinette or heel stitch until the flap is as long as the back of your heel.

To turn the heel, p to the midpoint of the flap, p 2 more, p 2 tog, p 1; then, without working the rest of that row, turn your work.

Sl 1 st, k an odd number of sts (usually 5 or so), k 2 tog, k1, and without finishing the row, turn your work again.

P across to one stitch before the gap made by the sl st, and then p tog the 2 sts on either side of the gap. Again, without finishing the row, turn your work.

Repeat these two rows, always slipping one stitch first, and knitting or purling the two stitches together at each side of the gap, until all the stitches are worked in one row, ending with a purl row. On the next row, knit half the stitches. This will bring you to the center of the heel. Put a "seam" marker here if you're knitting with four needles, and continue to the end of the heel stitches. Or if you have a five needle set, knit the remaining half of the heel stitches on their own needle.

Pick up stitches along the side of the heel, knit across the instep stitches (consolidating these onto one needle if you have only four needles), pick up stitches along the other side of the heel, and knit the first half of the heel stitches, bringing you back to the back seamline. You're now ready to knit the foot.

Begin toe shaping: Dec 4 sts each rnd as follows: Needles 1 and 3: K 1, sl 1, k 1 psso, work to end of needle. Needles 2 and 4: work to last 3 sts of needle, k 2 tog, k 1. Rep this dec rnd until 2 sts rem on each needle. Break off yarn and pull through each st. Pull tightly, sew in all loose ends into sock.

Socks for Brother, Mom, and Dad: Using colors as shown in photo, or substituting your own color changes, cast on 40 (48, 56) sts. Work 31 (30, 44) rnds of k 1, p 1 ribbing. Change to st st and work 3 rnds.

Heel: Keeping sts on needles 3 and 4 at rest for instep, work in rows of st st over rem sts for back of heel until 13 (20, 22) rows are completed. Turn heel as for little sister's socks, dec 1 st each side of center 8 (8, 10) heel sts until 8 (8, 10) sts are left. Pick up 8 (10, 12) sts each side of heel section, combine with instep sts, dec 1 st at beg and midpoint of rnd until same number of sts rem as were cast on. Work total of 40 (55, 53) rnds from ending of heel.

Begin toe shaping: Dec 1 st at beg of first and third needles and at end of second and fourth needles every rnd until 8 sts rem. Break off yarn and pull through each st. Pull tightly, sew in all loose ends into sock.

Classic Socks, *Gerda Amoraal*

KNITTING SOCKS brings back memories for Gerda Amoraal of Niagara Falls, Ontario. Her mother, who taught her to knit early, insisted that Gerda master this basic sock formula. By the time she was 16, Gerda could knit a sock while curled up reading a good book. Her mother, who was born in 1885, had learned to knit from her own mother; by the age of five, she was required to knit two rounds before she could go out to play. She could knit socks from memory by the time she was nine.

For the past six years, Gerda has combined her knitting skills with newly acquired spinning expertise. She's presently completing her Ontario Master Spinner course, with a special study in handspun angora. The version of her Classic Socks shown here was designed especially for her daughter Wendi, with a short cuff trimmed in angora.

For the intermediate knitter.

Size: Women's medium.

Yarn: 1200 yd/lb (2412 m/kg), 12 wraps/in (19/4 cm). Gerda used about 3 oz (85 g) handspun gray Shetland wool in a sport weight, and a small amount of handspun gray angora in a slightly finer weight.

Gauge: 7 sts = 1 in (11 sts = 4 cm).

Needles: Two sets of dpn, one each in size 1 (2.5 mm, 12) or size to reach gauge given above and in size 0 (2.25 mm, 13).

Instructions: (Editor's note: This pattern can be used for any number of sts, any length of foot, etc. The numbers given in parentheses refer to the socks shown in the photo.)

The Square Heel

This very angular heel turning is simple to keep track of, as all the rows are alike. Divide stitches and work a heel flap as for the Standard Heel, page 138, ending with a purl row.

To turn the heel, knit to the center, and then knit 3 stitches more (for a seven-stitch sole panel). Turn work. Purl 7, p 2 tog, turn. Knit 7, k 2 tog, turn. Continue in this way until all the stitches have been knitted in one row. Then proceed as for the Standard Heel.

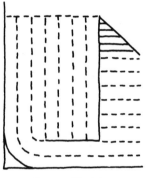

Square Shaping

On smaller needles cast on even number of sts needed for cuff (48). Work k 1, p 1 rib for desired length (1 ½ in, or 4 cm). Change to larger size needles, and work in st st for approximately 1 in (2 ½ cm). (Socks shown used angora for this inch.)

Heel flap: Divide sts as follows: First needle half of total number of sts (24), divide rem sts on rem 2 needles (12 on each needle).

Keeping sts on 2nd and 3rd needles in reserve for instep, work on sts of first needle in st st until there is 1 fewer row than number of sts on the needle (23 rows).

Turn heel:

Row 1: With wrong side facing, p to 1 st beyond the center point of row, p 2 tog, p 1, turn.

Row 2: Sl 1, k to one st past center, sl 1, k 1, psso, k 1, turn.

Row 3: Sl 1, p to one st before turning, p 2 tog, p 1, turn.

Row 4: Sl 1, k to one st before turning, sl 1, k 1, psso, k 1, turn. Rep Rows 3 and 4 until all sts are used. The last row will be a right side row and will have half the number of sts at beg of small heel plus 2 (14 sts).

With right side still facing, pick up 1 st in every other row along left edge of large heel, continue around working instep sts on 2nd and 3rd needles, pick up same number of sts along right edge of large heel as on left edge. Work even 1 rnd.

Instep shaping:

Rnd 1: Needle 1 (heel): Knit. Needle 2: Sl 1, k 1, psso, k to end of needle. Needle 3: K to last 2 sts, k 2 tog.

Rnd 2: Work even 1 rnd.

Rep these last 2 rnds until you have the same number of sts as cast on for cuff (48).

Knit the foot to the desired length (62 rows).

Toe shaping: Divide sts as for heel shaping. (24 sts on first needle, 12 on each of rem 2 needles).

Rnd 1: Needle 1: K 1, sl 1, k 1 psso, k to last 3 sts of needle, k 2 tog, k 1. Needle 2: K 1, sl 1, k 1, psso, k to end of needle. Needle 3: K to last 3 sts, k 2 tog, k 1.

Rnd 2: Next rnd: Knit. Rep these 2 rnds until half of the sts rem (24 sts). Rep dec rnd every rnd until there are 6 sts left; sew them tog.

A Trio of Festive Socks, *Theresa Gaffey*

LOTS OF experience with refining details went into these three sock variations by Theresa Gaffey of Atlanta, Georgia. Theresa's designs have appeared in most of the popular knitting publications, and she was knitting editor of *Handmade* magazine for a number of years.

Theresa has incorporated a sturdy heel stitch for sock longevity, and worked in a variety of pattern stitches for looks that range from sturdy to dressy to downright ebullient. She recommends *The Mitten Book* (Sterling/Lark) as a pattern source that will keep you trying new variations indefinitely.

Ribbed Sock

For the intermediate knitter.

Size: Adult medium.

Yarn: 1000 yd/lb (2010 m/kg), 11 wraps/in (17/4 cm). Theresa used 2 4-oz (113 g) skeins knitting worsted weight yarn, MC (red); 1 4-oz (113 g) skein knitting worsted weight yarn, CC (only 1 or 2 oz, or 30–50 g, of the green is required).

Gauge: Over st st with Size 4 needles 11 sts = 2 in (8½ sts = 4 cm).

Needles: One set of dpn, size 4 (3.5 mm, 9) or size to reach gauge given above; optional, one size 8 (5–5.5 mm, 5) needle.

Instructions: Ribbing pat (multiple of 4 sts): (K 2, p 2) around. Rep rnd for pat.

Cuff: With Size 8 needle or two Size 4 needles held tog and MC, cast on 52 sts. (Note: Cast-on row must be loose enough to stretch easily.) Divide sts on 3 needles as follows: 17, 18, 17. Join, being careful not to twist sts; mark beg of rnd. Work in k 2, p 2 ribbing for approximately 8 in (20 cm). Remove marker, k 2, replace marker for beg of rnd.

Divide for heel: The 52 sts should be divided in half as follows: 26 sts on first needle for heel; divide rem 26 sts on other two needles for top of foot. This division allows the sts allocated to top of foot to beg and end with k 2.

Heel flap: Change to CC. To make a firmer, more durable heel, work 26 heel sts in heel stitch until heel flap measures 2 to 2¼ in (5–6 cm), ending with a right side row.

Turn heel: The heel is turned by working a series of short rows out from center of heel flap as follows, slipping first st of each short row beg with Row 2:

Row 1: P to 2 sts beyond center of heel flap; that is, p first 15 sts, p next 2 sts tog, p 1, turn. Do not finish row.

Row 2: Sl first st, k 5, ssk, k 1, turn.

Row 3: Sl first st, p 6, p 2 tog, p 1. turn.

Work short rows in this manner, working one more st before dec each row, until all sts have been worked; 16 sts rem. End with a k row.

Shape instep: Break off contrasting color and attach main color. Using same (heel flap) needle, pick up 13 sts along left edge of heel flap. Keeping in ribbing pat, work

---

Heel Stitch

For extra-thick, long-wearing heels on your handknitted socks, use this simple pattern for the heel flaps:

Row 1: (outside row, on an even number of sts) Sl 1, k 1 across.

Row 2: sl 1, p across. Repeat these two rows for the length of the flap, ending with a plain knit row.

* * *

Even if you're knitting a plain stockinette flap, it's a good idea to slip the first stitch in each row. You'll find that picking up stitches along the sides of the flap is much easier.

across top of foot, transferring these 26 sts to one needle. With a third needle, pick up 13 sts along second heel flap edge and k first 8 sts of heel—68 sts. Place marker here for new beg of rnd.

Instep dec: Beg working again in rnds with 21 sts on first needle, 26 sts on second needle, and 21 sts on third—68 sts. Top of sock should be kept in ribbing pat; bottom should be kept in st st. Work 1 rnd even. On next rnd, dec as follows: K across first needle to last 2 sts, k 2 tog; work even across second needle; at beg of 3rd needle, ssk. Rep these last 2 rnds until 52 sts rem.

Work even in established pats until foot measures 2 in (5 cm) less than desired length.

Shape toe: Break off main color and with CC only, k 1 rnd even. Dec on next rnd as follows: Work to last 3 sts of first needle, k 2 tog, k 1; at beg of 2nd needle k 1, ssk, k to last 3 sts of 2nd needle, k 2 tog, k 1; at beg of third needle, k 1, ssk; complete rnd. Work even 1 rnd. Rep these last 2 rnds dec 4 sts every other rnd until 16 sts rem. Break off yarn, leaving a 12 in (30 cm) tail. Place sts of first and third needle to one needle; there are now 8 sts on each of 2 needles. Weave sts tog using kitchener stitch (page 39).

Lace Ankle Sock

For the intermediate knitter.

Size: Adult medium.

Yarn: 2400 yd/lb (4824 m/kg), 18 wraps/in (28/4 cm). Theresa used 2 50-g balls white fingering weight yarn.

Gauge: Over eyelet pat and Size 1 needles 8 sts = 1 in (12½ sts = 4 cm).

Needles: One set of dpn, size 1 (2.5mm, 12) or size to reach gauge given above.

Instructions: Eyelet pat (multiple of 6 sts):

> **Rnds 1, 3 and 5:** (P 1, k 5) around.
>
> **Rnd 2:** * P 1, k 1 yo, sl 1 as to k, k 2 tog, psso, yo, k 1; rep from * around.
>
> **Rnd 4:** * P 1, k 2, yo, ssk, k 1; rep from * around.
>
> **Rnd 6:** Rep Rnd 1. Rep Rnds 1–6 for pat.

Cuff: Cast on 72 sts loosely. (Note: The cast-on row must be loose enough to stretch easily; if necessary, cast on over two needles held tog.) Divide these sts evenly on 3 needles. Join, being careful not to twist sts; mark for beg of rnd. Work around in k 2, p 2 rib for approximately 3 in (8 cm).

Change to eyelet pat and work even for 4½ in (11 cm), approximately 10 reps of eyelet pat, ending with Rnd 5.

Divide for heel: Divide 72 sts as follows, adjusting sts so eyelet pat is centered on top of foot: 37 sts on one needle for heel; divide rem 35 sts on 2 needles for top of foot.

Heel flap: Dec 1 st at beg of first row, begin heel st over rem 36 sts, leaving sts for top of foot at rest. Work in heel stitch (page 141) until flap measures 2¼ in (6 cm), ending with a right-side row.

A TRIO OF FESTIVE SOCKS

Turn heel: Work series of short rows out from center of heel flap. First st of each short row is slipped beg with Row 2:

> **Row 1:** P to first st beyond center of heel flap; that is, p the first 19 sts, p next 2 sts tog, p 1, turn. Do not finish row.
>
> **Row 2:** Sl first st, k 3, ssk, k 1, turn.
>
> **Row 3:** Sl first st, p 4, p 2 tog, p 1, turn. Work short rows in this manner working one more st before dec every row until all sts have been worked ending with a k row—20 sts rem.

Shape instep: Using same (heel flap) needle, pick up 17 sts along left edge of heel flap. Keeping in eyelet pat, work across top of foot, transferring these 35 sts to one needle. With third needle, pick up 17 sts along second heel flap edge and k first 10 sts of heel—89 sts. Place marker here for beg of rnd.

Beg working again in rnds with 27 sts on first needle, 35 sts on second needle and 27 sts on third needle. Keep top of foot in eyelet pat, bottom of foot in st st. Work even 1 rnd. On next rnd, dec as follows: Work across first needle to last 2 sts, k 2 tog; work even across second needle; third needle: SSK, complete rnd. Rep these last 2 rnds until 69 sts rem.

Work even in established pats until foot measures 2 in (5 cm) less than desired length.

Shape toe: Discontinue eyelet pat, k 1 rnd, dec 1 st on second needle—68 sts. Dec on next rnd as follows: Work to 3 sts from end of first needle, k 2 tog, k 1; second needle: K 1, ssk, work to last 3 sts of second needle, k 2 tog, k 1; Third needle: K 1, ssk; complete rnd. Work 1 rnd even. Rep these last 2 rnds dec 4 sts every other rnd until 24 sts rem. Break off yarn, leaving a 12 in (30 cm) tail. Place sts of first and third needle on one needle—12 sts on each of two needles.

Join sts using kitchener stitch (page 39).

Finishing: Weave in loose ends and steam lightly.

Holiday Socks

For the intermediate knitter.

Size: Adult medium.

Yarn: 1000 yd/lb (2010 m/kg), 11 wraps/in (17/4 cm). Theresa used 2 4-oz (113 g) skeins knitting worsted weight yarn, one each of red and green.

Gauge: Over pat st 13 sts = 2 in (10 sts = 4 cm).

Needles: One set of dpn, size 7 (4.5–5 mm, 6) or size to reach gauge given above.

Instructions: Cuff: With red loosely cast on 60 sts. (Note: The cast-on row must be loose enough to stretch easily; if necessary, cast on over two needles held together.) Divide these sts evenly on 3 needles. Join, being careful not to twist sts; mark beg of rnd. Work in k 1, p 1 rib for approximately ½ in (1¼ cm). Change to st st, join green and work chart 1 for 4 rnds. Then work 2 rnds in red. Beg chart 2, rep 16 rows of chart as needed, working until sock measures 7 in (18 cm).

Divide for heel: The 60 sts should be divided as follows: 30 sts for top of foot; 30 sts for heel. Adjust division of sts to center color pat on top of foot. Sl heel sts to one needle and sl rem 30 sts to two needle.

Heel flap: Leaving 30 sts for top of foot at rest, change to red and work rem 30 sts in heel st until heel flap measure 2 in (5 cm), ending with a right-side row.

Turn heel: Work series of short rows out from center of heel flap. First st of each short row is slipped beg with Row 2.

  Row 1: P to 2 sts beyond center of heel flap; that is, p first 17 sts, p next 2 sts tog, p 1, turn. Do not finish row.

  Row 2: Sl first st, k 5, ssk k 1, turn.

  Row 3: Sl first st, p 6, p 2 tog, p 1, turn.

Work short rows in this manner, working one more st before dec every row until all sts have been worked, ending with a k row—18 sts remain.

Shape gusset: Attach green and using same (heel flap) needle pick up 14 sts along left edge of heel flap, following chart 3. Keeping top of foot in color pat 2 as established, work across top of foot, transferring these 30 sts to one needle. With a third needle, pick up 14 sts along right edge of heel flap and k first 9 sts of heel—76 sts. Place marker for beg of rnd.

Begin working in rnds with 23 sts on first needle, 30 sts on second needle and 23 sts on third needle. Keeping top of sock in pat 2, bottom and gusset in pat 3, work 1 rnd even. Next rnd: Dec as follows: Work to last 2 sts of first needle, k 2 tog; work across second needle, third needle: ssk, complete rnd. Rep these last 2 rnds until 56 sts rem.

Work even in pats as established until foot measures 2 in (5 cm) less than desired length.

Shape toe: Break off green and with red only, work 1 rnd. Dec on next rnd as follows: Work to last 3 sts of first needle, k 2 tog, k 1; second needle: k 1, ssk, work to last 3 sts of needle, k 2 tog, k 1; third needle: k 1, ssk; complete rnd. Work 1 rnd even. Rep these last 2 rnds dec 4 sts every other rnd until 16 sts rem. Break off yarn, leaving 12 in (30 cm) tail. Place sts of first and third needle on one needle; there are 8 sts on each of two needles.

Weave sts tog using kitchener stitch (page 39).

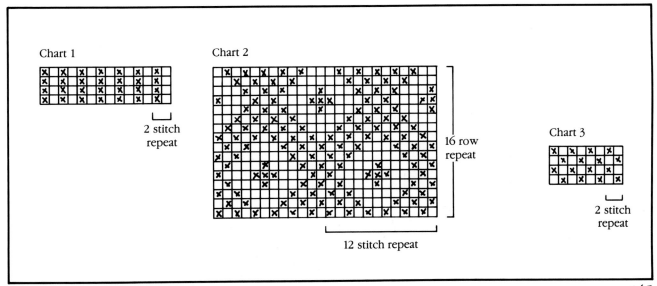

Chart 1

2 stitch repeat

Chart 2

16 row repeat

12 stitch repeat

Chart 3

2 stitch repeat

Slipper Socks, *Joan Lawler*

WHAT IN Joan Lawler's background prepared her for knitting 400 pairs of these cozy slippers? A Canadian emigrant to England, Joan trained in a New York art school, and later served as art editor on a women's magazine. She recently assumed ownership of a spinning supply business, and has set production knitting aside.

Her inspiration for this design was a great number of small balls of handspun yarn, and three small grandsons who couldn't keep their slippers on. She wanted a non-skid sole, and was lucky to find off-cuts from a sheepskin coat factory at a reasonable price. One thing led to another, and she soon found herself making the slippers in 13 different sizes—and selling them as fast as she could knit them up.

The slipper soles are cut from scrap leather, holes are punched around the edge, and a few rows of crochet set the stage for the knitted tops.

For the intermediate knitter.

Size: Small (child size 1). Changes for child's sizes medium and large (2 and 3) follow in parentheses.

Yarn: 1400 yd/lb (2814 m/kg), 12–14 wraps/in (19–22/4 cm). Joan's yarns are 2-ply handspuns in a fluffy sport weight. If using commercial yarns, try a knitting worsted weight. She used about 2 (3, 3) oz (56–85 g) handspun wool in three colors: MC (main color), CC (contrast color), S (sole color).

Gauge: Over stockinette st, 4 sts = 1 in (6 sts = 4 cm).

Needles: Two sets of dpn, one each in size 8 (5–5.5 mm, 5) or size to reach gauge given above and in size 6 (4–4.5 mm, 7); two crochet hooks, one each in size C or 2 (2.75–3 mm, 11), and in size E or 4 (3.5 mm, 9).

Miscellaneous materials: 1 pair sheepskin soles with 26 (26, 28) holes punched. See diagram.

Instructions: Rnd 1: With smaller crochet hook and S and with suede side of sheepskin facing, join with sl st to center heel of sole, ch 2, * sc in next hole, ch 1; rep from * around. Join with sl st to top of beg ch-2.

Rnd 2: With larger hook, ch 2; work sc in each ch-1 sp of previous rnd to end of rnd. Join with sl st to top of beg ch-2. Fasten off.

Rnd 3: With same hook and CC, join bet sc of previous rnd; ch 2. Work dc in each sp bet sc of previous rnd. Join with sl st in top of beg ch-2. Fasten off.

Rnd 4: With same hook and S draw lp bet dc of previous rnd; ch 1. Sc in each sp bet dc of previous rnd. Join with sl st in top of first ch.

Begin knitting: *Note:* When picking up sts from crocheted edge, pick up through single lp at inside edge of row.

Row 1: With one of the Size 6 needles, MC and right side facing, pick up and k 4 sts at the center of the toe, turn.

Row 2: Purl across the toe sts, pick up 1 st at end of the row—5 sts. Turn.

Row 3: Knit, picking up 1 st at end of row—6 sts. Turn.

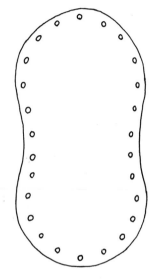

Trace around foot, adding plenty of ease.

Row 4: Purl 5, purling 2 tog at end of row using 1 lp from crochet row for 2nd st. Turn.

Row 5: K 5, knitting 2 tog at end of row using lp of crochet as second st. Turn.

Row 6: Rep Row 4.

Size small only:

Row 7: K 6, pick up 1 st by knitting through lp of crochet at end of row—7 sts.

Row 8: Purl 7, purl through crochet lp at end of row—8 sts.

Row 9: K 8; with another needle, pick up and k next 9 crochet lps. With another needle k next 9 lps from crochet, then knit across the instep and k first 9 sts. You are now at the center of the heel and this is the new beg of work, now worked in rnds—26 sts.

Rnds 10 and 11: Work even.

Rnd 12: K 1, sl 1, k 1, psso, k 6—25 sts. Turn.

Rnd 13: K 6, k 2 tog, k 19—24 sts.

Rnds 14-15: Work even.

Sizes medium and large:

Row 7: Rep Row 5.

Row 8: Rep Row 4.

Row 9: K 6, pick up 1 through lp of crochet at end of row—7 sts.

Row 10: Purl 7, pick up 1—8 sts.

Row 11: K 8, With another needle pick up and k next 9 (10) back lp of crochet. With another needle k next 9 (10) lp from crochet, then k across instep and k first 9 (10) sts. You should now be at the center of the heel and this is the new beg of rnd 26—(28) sts.

Rnds 12 and 13: Work even

Rnd 14: K 19 (20) sts, sl 1, k 1, psso, k 5 (6)—25 (27) sts.

Rnd 15: K 6 (7), k 2 tog, k 17 (18)—24 (26) sts.

Rnds 16-18: Work even.

Size large only: Rnd 19: Work even.

All sizes: Change to larger needles and work in k 1, p 1 rib for 16 (18, 20) rnds. To cast off use very much larger needle in right hand to give correct looseness in casting off.

Rainbow Knee Socks, *Betty Amos*

"SOME LEGS," Betty Amos muses, "are shaped like baseball bats, and some resemble Thanksgiving turkey drumsticks. So it's no great wonder that the fit of manufactured knee socks often leaves a bit to be desired. To look well, fit well, and stay up without tight garters, they should be designed to fit the prospective wearer." With the aid of a few measurements, a gauge swatch, and some simple arithmetic, success will be forthcoming.

Betty cautions that, since there is often a difference of several inches between the calf and ankle circumference, a lot of decreases will have to be made within a vertical distance of only six inches or less. She lines her decreases up in pairs on either side of a center back "seamline" that's several stitches wide. The seamline can be plain, or patterned as in Elizabeth Zimmermann's "Wearable Art Socks", page 154.

Betty's Rainbow Knee Socks get their distinctive look from corrugated ribbing (see page 62) worked in a plain yarn and a variegated one. Corrugated ribbing is thicker and less elastic than regular k 2, p 2 ribbing, but these socks are so nicely shaped that they stay up reliably and flatter the wearer.

For the intermediate knitter.

Size: Women's medium.

Yarn: 1200 yd/lb (2412 m/kg), 15 wraps/in (13/4 cm). Betty's yarns are 2-ply sport-weight handspuns; she used 6 oz (170 g) of natural gray, and 5 oz (142 g) variegated "rainbow" yarn from dyed wool.

Gauge: Over corrugated rib 8 sts= 1 in (12 sts= 4 cm).

Needles: Two sets of five dpn, size 1 (2.25 mm, 12) and size 2 (2.75 mm, 13).

Instructions: With smaller needles and gray yarn, cast on 96 sts, or sufficient (multiple of 4) to fit comfortably around leg just below knee. Work in k 2, p 2 rib for 2 in (5 cm).

Change to larger needles and join rainbow yarn and continue in rib as established, working k 2 with gray yarn and p 2 with rainbow yarn until total length measures approximately 7 in (18 cm) or reaches point where leg begins to dec in circumference, ending 2 sts before end of rnd. (Ed note: Because yarn is being carried across wrong side of work, this will stabilize the rib and reduce some of its natural elasticity.)

Place marker (this becomes beg of rnd), p 2, k 2, p 2, place second marker.

Calf shaping: Keeping 6 sts bet markers in rib pat as established, dec 2 sts before first marker and after second marker on next rnd. Following rnd, rep dec. Work even for approximately 1 in (2.5 cm). Rep 2 dec rnds every in (2.5 cm) until 64 sts rem, or sufficient to reach comfortably around ankle, leaving a multiple of 4 sts. Work even to top of heel. Break off rainbow yarn at beg of 3rd needle.

Heel flap: Leaving center half of sts at rest on first 2 needles for instep, work on 32 sts of other two needles in Heel Stitch:

> **Row 1:** Sl 1, k 1 across.
>
> **Row 2:** P across.

Work in this way until flap measures 2½ in (6.5 cm), ending with a k row.

Turn heel:

  Row 1: P 18, p 2 tog, p 1, turn.

  Row 2: Sl 1, k 5, sl 1, k 1, psso, k 1, turn.

  Row 3: Sl 1, p 6, p 2 tog, p 1, turn.

  Row 4: Sl 1, k 7, sl 1, k 1, psso, k 1, turn.

Continue in this way, working one more st each time, until all sts have been worked, ending with a k row. Break off yarn. There should be 9 sts each on the 1st and 4th needles, and 16 sts each on the 2nd and 3rd needles.

Heel gusset: On 1st needle, pick up 15 sts along side edge of heel flap. On 4th needle, pick up 15 sts from other side of heel flap. There will now be 24 sts on 1st needle, 16 sts on 2nd needle, 16 sts on 3rd needle, and 24 sts on 4th needle. Tie in gray yarn at beg of 1st needle, k 2, tie in rainbow yarn, p 2, and continue in pattern to end of 4th needle.

Heel gusset decrease:

  Rnd 1: work in pat across 20 sts of 1st needle, k 2 tog (gray), p 2 (rainbow). Continue in pat across 2nd and 3rd needles. Beg 4th needle with k 2 gray, p 2 rainbow tog, work in pat to end of rnd.

  Rnd 2: Work in pat around; at decs, k the k sts and p the p sts.

Continue in this way, decreasing 1 st every other rnd in each heel gusset until only 16 sts rem on 1st and 4th needles (64 sts rem).

Foot: Work in pat on 64 sts until 6½ in (16.5 cm) from heel, or desired length minus 2½ in (6 cm). Break off rainbow yarn.

Toe decrease: Dec 1 st at end of 1st needle and beg of 2nd needle, and at end of 3rd needle and beg of 4th needle. Work next rnd plain. Continue working these 2 rnds until there are only 5 sts left on each needle. Weave these tog (page 39) to close toe.

Shaping a Knee Sock

You can custom fit your knee socks so that they never sag by taking note of some simple vertical dimensions, as suggested by Betty Amos. Here are her sample measurements; vary them to suit the legs for which you're knitting.

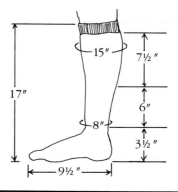

---

x

RAINBOW KNEE SOCKS

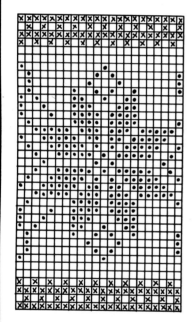

A Christmas Stocking, *Linda Ligon*

AS EDITOR of this book, I wanted to take the opportunity to include a pattern of my own. But as the old saying goes, "Those that can, knit. Those that can't, edit." Or something like that. I've been knitting for years, but have made more than my share of hats that are too tight, mittens that are slightly different in size, and—worst of all—socks which never had a mate. There's something about knitting the same thing twice that simply defeats me. I remember starting a pair of socks for my (now) husband when we were dating. Christmas Eve came too soon, and I had to give him half a pair, with an appeasing note:

> Within this box is just one sock
> Which I have knit for you.
> For though I knit, and knit, and knit,
> I never did get through.

Twenty-five years later, that one lone, tatty sock still hangs on the mantel by itself each yuletide, having found a use.

Given that I have this problem with pairs, some of the happiest knitting I've done over the years is one-of-a-kind, over-size Christmas stockings for my kids. The first one was an experiment, very plain and simple. By the time I got to number three, I had confidence: it is a jolly, tasteless riot of every Fair Isle pattern I could lay hands on that fit my number of stitches. What you see here is number two. It's basically just a standard sock, but knitted in fat yarn on big needles. It's a little unusual in that you have to sew up the gussets after you're finished. I don't like to pick up stitches, either.

For the intermediate knitter.

Size: Leg, 18 in (46 cm) long, foot, 14 in (36 cm) long.

Yarn: 1000 yd/lb (2010 m/kg), 11 wraps/in (17/4 cm). Four-ply knitting worsted-type yarn, one 4 oz (114 g) skein white; 1 oz (28 g) red, few yards of green.

Gauge: Over stockinette st 5 sts = 1 in (8 sts = 4 cm).

Needles: One set dpn size 6 (4–4.5 mm, 7) or size to reach gauge given above.

Instructions: Leg: With white cast on 66 sts; join and place marker for beg of rnd (center back). Work k 1, p 1 rib for 2 in (5 cm). Change to st st, work 2 rnds, then beg chart. When chart is completed, continue in st st with white until piece measures 14 in (36 cm) from beg of ribbing.

Divide for heel: Work first 17 sts and sl to holder for heel, work center 32 sts for instep; sl rem 17 sts to second holder for heel.

Instep: Work back and forth on 32 instep sts in st st for 21 rows ending with a p row. Sl these instep sts to holder.

Heel flap: Move 34 heel sts from two holders to one needle. With wrong side facing, join red.

Row 1 (wrong side): Sl 1, p 2 tog, p across to last 2 sts, p 2 tog—32 sts.

Row 2: * Sl 1, k 1; rep from * across.

Row 3: Sl 1, p to end of row.

Rep Rows 2 and 3 until there are 27 rows of heel in all.

Turn heel:

Row 1 (right side): K 17, k 2 tog, k 1, turn.

Row 2: Sl 1, p 4, p 2 tog, p 1, turn.

Row 3: Sl 1, k 5, k 2 tog, k 1, turn.

Row 4: Sl 1, p 6, p 2 tog, p 1, turn.

Continue in this way working one more st bet decs until all sts have been worked, ending with a purl row—17 sts remain. Break off red.

Instep shaping: With right side facing and with white, pick up and k 15 sts along right edge of heel, k across 17 heel sts, pick up and k 15 sts along left edge of heel—47 sts.

Row 1: Purl.

Row 2: K 1, sl 1, k 1, psso, k to last 3 sts, k 2 tog, k 1.

Rep these last 2 rows until 29 sts rem. P 1 row, k 1 row.

Foot: Place 29 heel sts and 32 instep sts on 3 dpn—61 sts. First heel st is beg of rnd. K on 61 sts for 40 rnds, dec 1 st on last rnd—60 sts. Break off white; join red.

Shape toe:

Rnd 1: (K 2 tog, k 26, k 2 tog) twice—56 sts.

Rnd 2: Knit.

Rnd 3: (K 2 tog, k 24, k 2 tog) twice—52 sts.

Rnd 4: Knit.

Rep Rnds 3 and 4, having 2 fewer sts bet decs every other rnd, until 20 sts rem. Weave toe sts tog using kitchener stitch (page 39).

Finishing: Steam press sock. Sew gusset seams.

Wearable Art Sock, *Elizabeth Zimmermann*

WHEN IS A sock much more than a sock? When it's Elizabeth's fanciful, structurally interesting "art sock". "For the hostess to wear, shoeless, with her feet up on the coffee table," she says. What makes these socks architecturally intriguing is the shaping: paired increases along the top of the instep mirror paired decreases right down the middle of the arch. If you can't visualize it, take it on faith—it works. A whimsical bonus is the turned-up toe; and a knitted cord laces jauntily through the top ribbing for decoration and stay-up security.

For the intermediate knitter.

Size: Women's medium.

Yarn: 840 yd/lb (1688 m/kg), 12 wraps/in (19/4 cm). Elizabeth has used 6–8 oz (170–226 g) 2-ply Sheepswool in cream (MC), and 3–4 oz (85–113 g) of dark red (CC).

Gauge: Over stockinette st, 6 sts= 1 in (9 sts= 4 cm).

Needles: Circular needle, 16 in (40 cm) long, and one set dpn, both size 5 (3.75 mm, 8), or size to reach gauge given above.

Instructions: With 16 in (40 cm) needle and MC cast on 60 sts. Join and work twisted rib (k 1 in back loop, p 1) for 15 rnds. Change to st st and inc to 70 sts in first rnd: (K 6, M1) around. Establish the pattern for the stocking, marking off the leftover sts at the beg of the rnd for the center back "seam". Work straight until the total length is 7 in (18 cm).

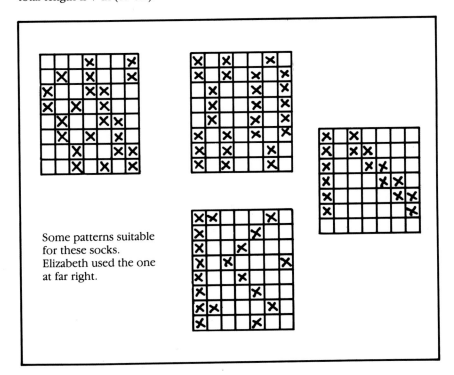

Some patterns suitable for these socks. Elizabeth used the one at far right.

Calf shaping: Dec 1 st each side of "seam" sts every 4th rnd: K 2 tog, k "seam", SSK. Continue to dec until you have 58 sts. Work straight to ankle (about 16 in or 40 cm total length).

Foot shaping: Mark about 3 sts at the center front for inset "seam" directly opposite back "seam." Inc 1 st each side of inset "seam" every rnd by M1. This top-of-foot shaping continues to the bitter end—or can be discontinued for the last 2-3 rnds, if you prefer a less pointed toe.

When stocking is about 18 in (46 cm) long, has about 2 in (5 cm) worth of instep shaping and has a total of about 82-84 sts, begin heel shaping.

Heel shaping: Dec 1 st each side of center back "seam" sts every rnd (K 2 tog, k "seam", SSK) for 9 rnds. Now place 22 center back sts on a thread (to be woven later) and continue around (on about 60 sts), still inc at instep and dec at sole until foot is wanted length. Weave remaining sts, which will make a cute pointed toe, and weave sts at arch of foot.

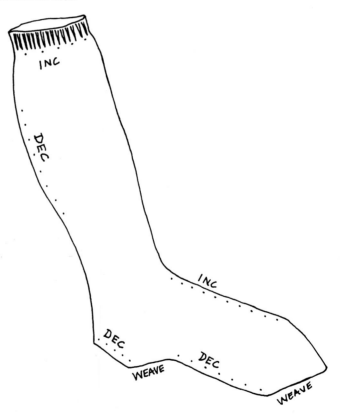

The above directions are an amalgamation of the 4 or 5 models my daughter and I knitted up; no two are exactly alike, so don't feel bound to the above numbers.

WEARABLE ART SOCK

Wee Socks, *Theresa Gaffey*

YOU'LL THINK of a dozen uses for these quick to knit miniatures: package decorations, finger dancers, doll footwear, shoelace tassels. Not least, if you've never knitted socks before, these are made just like the real thing—you can learn the concepts of heel turning and toe shaping without investing a lot of time and yarn. Knitted from bits of fingering yarn on #1 needles, the pattern possibilities are limited only by your scrap bag and the 20 stitch round.

Whether you stick to tiny projects like this one, or tackle the grandest challenge you can imagine, may you find joy in creating good cloth, and serenity in the rhythm of the needles.

For the beginning knitter.

Size: About 3 in (7–8 cm) from cuff to toe.

Yarn: 1500 yd/lb (1371 m/kg), 18 wraps/in (28/4 cm). Theresa used scraps of fingering-weight yarn in two colors; only a few yards are needed for each sock.

Gauge: 8 sts = 1 in (12–13/4 cm).

Needles: One set dpn 7 in (18 cm) long, size 1 (2.5 mm, 13).

Instructions: *Loosely* cast on 20 sts. Divide these sts between 3 needles. Join, being careful not to twist sts, and mark the beg of the rnd. Work k 1, p 1 ribbing for 3 rnds.

Change to stockinette st; work in color stripes or pattern of your choice until sock measures 1¾ in (4.5 cm).

Divide for heel: Place 5 sts on each of two needles for top of foot, and 10 sts on the other needle for the heel flap. If the small size of the sock makes working the heel difficult, place the foot sts on a holder or string to keep them out of the way.

Heel flap: Change to contrasting color and work in st st for ½ in (1.25 cm), ending with a right-side row.

Turn heel: Row 1: P to center of the heel flap; p next 2 sts tog, p 1, turn.
    Row 2: Sl 1, k 1, ssk, k 1, turn.
    Row 3: Sl 1, p 2, p 2 tog, p 1, turn.
    Row 4: Sl 1, k 3, ssk, k 1, turn—6 sts rem.

Shape instep: Attach mc and using the same heel flap needle, pick up 4 sts along left edge of heel flap. Work across top of foot, transferring these 10 sts onto one needle. With a third needle, pick up 4 sts along second heel flap edge and k first 3 sts of heel. Place marker here for beg of rnd.

Work in rnds, adjusting sts so there are 8 on each needle—24 sts total. Work 1 rnd even. On next rnd, dec as follows: at end of first needle, k 2 tog. Work even across second needle. At beg of third needle, ssk. Rep these 2 rnds until 16 sts rem. Work 2 rnds even or until foot measures ½ in (1.25 cm) less than desired length.

Shape toe: Attach cc, k 1 rnd even. Dec on next rnd as follows: At end of first needle k last 2 sts tog. At beg of second needle, ssk. At end of second needle, k 2 tog. At beg of third needle, ssk. Work 1 rnd even. Rep these two rnds, dec 4 sts every other rnd, until 8 sts rem. Break off yarn, leaving a 5 in (12 cm) tail. Place sts of first and third needles on one needle. There should now be 4 sts on each of two needles. Weave toe using kitchener stitch (page 39).

Resource Guide

Fibers and Special Tools

Here is a list of some of the suppliers whose products were used in various projects throughout the book. Look for their yarns and tools at your local knitting or weaving shop, or write the manufacturer for a dealer in your area.

Alden Amos, 11178 Upper Previtali Road, Jackson, CA 95642. "Rainbow wool batts for handspinning variegated yarns.

Brunswick Worsted Mills, Inc., Moosup, CT 06354. Icelandic Lopi and Pomfret sport-weight yarns.

Condon & Sons Ltd., P.O. Box 129, Charlottetown, Prince Edward Island, Canada C1A 7K3.

Eaton Yarns, c/o Craft Skellar, Marymount College, Tarytown, NY 10591. Helmi Vuorelma Oy Finnish yarns as used in Lizbeth Upitis' Cathedral Mittens.

Grandor Industries, 716 E. Valley Parkway, Unit 48H, Escondido, CA 92025. Supplier of the McMorran Yarn Balance.

Harrisville Designs, P.O. Box 281, Harrisville, NH 03450. Knitting yarns, and weaving yarns suitable for knitting, as used in Jackie Fee's Mushroom Cap and Mittens.

Ironstone Yarns, P.O. Box 196, Uxbridge, MA 01569. English mohair.

Schoolhouse Press, 6899 Cary Bluff, Pittsville, WI 54466. Meg Swansen's unspun Icelandic wool, Sheepswool knitting yarns, books and tools.

Patons, Susan Bates Inc., 212 Middlesex Ave., Chester, CT 06412. Dorothy Petersen used a Patons yarn in her Simply Dressy Hat.

Pingouin Corporation, P.O. Box 100, Jamestown, SC 29453. Fingering yarn as used in Jean Scorgie's Baby Cap.

Reynolds Yarns, Inc., P.O. Box 1776, Hauppauge, NY 11788. A primary supplier of Icelandic lopi-type yarns.

Schoolhouse Yarns, 25495 S.E. Hoffmeister Rd., Boring, OR 97009. Helmi Vuorelma Oy Finnish yarns as used in Lizbeth Upitis' Cathedral Mittens.

Sweater Workshop, The, P.O. Box 5, Hingham, MA 02043. Jackie Fee's mail-order books and knitting tools.

Tahki Yarn Imports Ltd., 92 Kennedy St., Hackensack, NJ 07801.

Books

Becker, Mary Lamb. *The Mitten Book.* Milwaukee: Reiman Publications, 1978.

Bliss, Anne. *A Handbook of Dyes From Natural Materials.* New York: Charles Scribner's Sons, 1981.

Buchanan, Rita. *A Weaver's Garden.* Loveland, Colorado: Interweave Press, Inc., 1987.

Fee, Jacqueline. *The Sweater Workshop.* Loveland, Colorado: Interweave Press, Inc., 1983.

Gottfridsson, Inger, and Ingrid Gottfridsson. *The Mitten Book.* New York: Sterling/Lark, 1985.

Hansen, Robin. *Fox & Geese & Fences: A Collection of Traditional Maine Mittens.* Camden, Maine: Down East Books, 1983.

Hansen, Robin, and Janetta Dexter. *Flying Geese and Partridge Feet.* Camden, Maine: Down East Books.

Haglund, Ulla, and Ingrid Mesterton. *Bohus Stickning.* Utgiven av Foreningen Bohus Stickning, 1980.

McGregor, Sheila. *The Complete Book of Traditional Fair Isle Knitting.* New York: Charles Scribner's Sons, 1982.

Norbury, Janes. *Traditional Knitting Patterns.* Dover.

Price, Lesley Anne. *Kids Knits.* New York: Ballentine, 1983.

Roberts, Priscilla-Gibson. *Knitting In the Old Way.* Loveland, Colorado: Interweave Press, Inc., 1985.

Royce, Beverly. *Notes On Double Knitting.* Published by the author, Rt. 1, Langdon, Kansas.

Thomas, Mary. *Mary Thomas' Knitting Book.* Dover Publications, 1972.

Walker, Barbara. *A Treasury of Knitting Patterns.*

-----. *A Second Treasury of Knitting Patterns.*

Zimmermann, Elizabeth. *Knitting Without Tears.* New York: Charles Scribner's Sons, 1971.

Magazines

Handwoven. Interweave Press, Inc., 201 E. 4th St., Loveland, CO 80537.

Spin·Off. Interweave Press, Inc., 201 E. 4th St., Loveland, CO 80537.

Vogue Knitting. 161 Avenue of the Americas, New York, NY 10013.

Wool Gathering. Schoolhouse Press, 6899 Cary Bluff, Pittsville, WI 54466.